D1027249

Growing Faith

GROWING FAITH

Bruce P. Powers

DISCARDED
JENKS LRC
GORDON COLLEGE

Wipf & Stock
PUBLISHERS
Eugene, Oregon

JENKS LIBRARY
GORDON COLLEGE
255 GRAPEVINE RD.
WENHAM, MA 01984

Wipf and Stock Publishers
199 West 8th Avenue, Suite 3
Eugene, Oregon 97401

Growing Faith
By Powers, Bruce P.
Copyright©1982 by Powers, Bruce P.
ISBN: 1-59244-430-X
Publication date: 12/3/2003
Previously published by Broadman Press, 1982

Scripture quotations marked RSV are from the Revised Standard Version of the Bible, copyrighted 1946, 1952, © 1971, 1973. Those marked TEV are from the *Good News Bible*, the Bible in Today's English Version. Old Testament: Copyright © American Bible Society 1976; New Testament: Copyright © American Bible Society 1966, 1971, 1976. Used by permission.

Dedicated to
my mother Lila
and the memory of my father Bruce,
parents who birthed me in faith,
nurtured me in family, and
set the example for Christian service.

Acknowledgments

Faculty and student colleagues have contributed much to my interest in and the development of this project.

Professors Bill Clemmons and Bob Poerschke have provided wise counsel and evoked pertinent thoughts.

Students over three years have participated with me in research by conducting surveys and interviews, interpreting faith development theories, and studying their own religious experiences. We have sought together to develop skills in growing faith in our own lives as well as in the lives of others. Those who participated in this project include:

Garry Baldwin
Pamela Bass
Carol Bastin
John Batchelor
Randell Blackman
Jim Brophy
Bruce Butts
Robin Coira
Diane Cole
Kenneth Cox
Lawrence Creedle
Brandon Deane
Claudia Forrest
James Hales
Floyd Hammond
Gary Hanna
Craig Hardee
Jeanne Hollifield
Robert Hylton
James Jacobs
Susan Joy
Philip Kent
Tim Kirkland

Dianne Lawrence
Kimberly Lee
Michael Lipe
Floyd Loftin
Jack Lutz
Gary McCollough
Tommy McDearis
Mike McKeown
Beth MacLeod
Frances McManus
Shirley Massey
Ronald Moore
Andy Morris
Frank Nuckolls
Nancy Ollis
Don Patty
Larry Pitts, Jr.
Judith Powell
Elizabeth Puckett
Chris Rackley
Brian Reynolds
James Reynolds
David Ricard

Bob Riley
Kenneth Robinson
Richard Rockwell, Jr.
Lee Scripture, Jr.
Francis Smith
Earl Spivey, Jr.
Ken Spivey
Robert Stalvey
Louis Strickland
Twila Thurm
David Troutman
Bill Truesdale, Jr.
Jeanine Tuten
Roger Underwood
Martha Vertrees
Carlton Walker
Jo Westbury
Kim Williams
Karen Wilson
Ann Wootton
Cathy York
Richard Young

Preface

I want to live my faith; and I want to pass it on. Of the issues in my life, this has become number one.

There are two primary reasons for this. First, in our churches we teachers, leaders, and parents *are* passing on faith. But what is the quality of this faith? Is faith a code of doctrines and liturgy, a way of living, or a quality of relationship with God in Christ? Yes, it is probably a combination; but with the abundance of religious viewpoints, who decides? *What will be the religious faith of the next generation?*

The other reason is the great plurality in cultural values, especially those related to concern and respect for others. Ours is a me/mine generation, with selfish interests creating not only economic and political barriers, but also religious boundaries.

With this apparent confusion in beliefs and practices among Christian institutions and in society, I must ask: *What is the faith we will pass on?*

This book began as a personal effort to answer this question for me and my family. But it quickly became much more. As I talked with people in churches, I found a great concern about the very problems I cited. Yet little was being done because the answers are so nebulous.

Growing Faith became a journey into the nature of Christian discipleship – how you get it, how you live it, and how you pass it on. It is a *people* study, for and about Christians who see growing faith as a distinctive quality of discipleship.

I offer it as a chance for you to enlarge your own faith as well as to develop skills in helping others. At the end of each chapter are learning activities which will provide additional guidance for individual or group study.

Because of their relevance, I have included some of my previously published materials. In chapters 2 and 5, portions have been drawn from *Christian Leadership* (Broadman Press, 1979) and from an audiotape, *Helping People Learn* (Broadman Press, 1978). In chapter 6, I have included an article reprinted from the Fall 1981 issue of *Living with Preschoolers,* a Christian family periodical published by the Sunday School Board, Nashville, Tennessee.

To my former faculty and student colleagues who encouraged this work when it was first published in 1982, I express my thanks. In the acknowledgments I listed those directly involved. Appreciation also is due Malcolm Atkins, Denise Donovan, Jeff Neuberger, and JoAnn Wright, my graduate assistants who helped compile the research, and my wife, Jean, who critiqued and proofed the work.

Students, faculty, and staff of the Campbell University Divinity School have assisted in the publication of this reprint edition. My colleague, Dean Michael G. Cogdill, our administrative assistant, Joyce Mashtare, and the faculty have been especially helpful as we have used the principles in this book in developing the spiritual formation components of the divinity school's curriculum. The founding purpose of the school, which began in 1996, is drawn from the theological images in *Growing Faith* – to be "Christ-centered, Bible-based, and Ministry-focused."

Bruce P. Powers
Campbell University Divinity School
Buies Creek, North Carolina

Contents

1
Faith Development as a Lifelong Process

I think faith has many channels. Only by going through each channel, even through several channels at a time, do we get the full meaning. I think different incidents in our lives will change our feelings on faith from an innocent childlike faith to a mature faith.

A childlike acceptance means God loves me and I love him and everything is going to be fine. Sometimes I slip back into this, and then at other times I want to be big and strong and put myself wholeheartedly into asking God just to back me up as I blast forth dynamically instead of relying on that childlike dependence.

Female, age 41
Married, five children

How would you describe faith? Is faith something you have, or something you do? Or is it what you believe?

Is there *a* faith or *the* faith, and is it personal? Or, perhaps, does it belong to a group or to a type of people?

How have you experienced faith? Of the religious issues I have faced as a middle-aged adult, this has been the most crucial. Whereas during young adult years I was preoccupied with how to be a Christian leader, my personal growth concerns have enlarged to focus on leadership and spiritual development.

As I recounted in *Christian Leadership*, my pilgrimage has led me to view God's will as being revealed primarily through *guidelines* and *principles* for Christian service rather than through specific instructions. So it appears with spiritual development: Jesus gave guidelines and examples for spiritual growth, but offered few details about exactly what to do and how to do it.

He avoided creating legal requirements such as the religious system of his day had developed, preferring to pose questions, parables, and illustrations that would require inquirers and followers to explore possibilities and determine a personalized response.

In my mind Jesus always pushed individuals to make their own specific application of his teachings, placing them in situations that required decisions and actions based on personal commitment. It is in these acts of human response to God that faith is exhibited, can be tested, and, through a continuing growth process, refined in the *likeness* of Jesus and his teachings. Never an exact copy, mind you, but a maturing and growing nature that reflects freedom of choice, personal commitment, and active response.

Do you want to explore the faith issue? Do you want to gain a better understanding of your spiritual development and how to help others in growing faith? Come, let me take you with me through the ideas and reflections, hopes and struggles, which have become dominant in my life over the last two years.

I hope you will suspend judgment about the rightness or wrongness about what I share with you. For, beyond personal opinion, there can be no final answer about faith or how it develops. There can be only descriptive information based on the interpretations and impressions gained as we have interacted with and responded to God. It is these insights which have been helpful to me, and which I wish to share with you. They are not *the* answer to growing faith, but only expressions of how persons have viewed spiritual development as they have experienced it. Examine these ideas, compare them with your experiences, then determine how best for *you* to pursue a continual journey toward Christlikeness.

WHAT IS FAITH?

Faith usually is defined as what a person believes. But it is much more; for example, what one *does* is also an expression of faith. Faith, in addition, requires elements of *why* and *how* I believe. In the past I usually have avoided explaining faith; it just is. Isn't that enough?

But at age forty-one, I can't stop asking questions and posing answers. So here is a possibility: Faith is an *interpretation* of the way persons have experienced life. This interpretation, drawn from all of the influences on our lives, is the essence of our beliefs, actions, and emotions. Faith, rather than being something we believe that can be compiled, taught, and tested, is more a *way* of knowing the unknowable.

By definition, faith is an expression of trust in the unknown. Where there is certainty—when everything can be explained and understood in human terms—there is no need for faith. Faith is my way of knowing that God exists, that Jesus is Lord as well as my personal redeemer, and that the Holy Spirit is the direct presence of God which infuses my life, empowers the church, and calls all humankind to a redemptive relationship.

Faith has degrees of understanding and conviction. I used to think that a person either had faith or did not. But then I realized that *everyone* has beliefs, and that these beliefs guide actions. It is not whether one has faith or not, but the *content* and the *quality* of the faith that ultimately is a part of every individual.

HOW DOES FAITH GROW?

The next question focuses on the pilgrim image long associated with Christians as illustrated in Ephesians 4:11-16. We are to grow into the likeness of Christ. How does a person develop as a disciple of Jesus Christ?

Where does a person begin in the faith, and what happens as a person experiences a growing faith? A beginning point, for example, might be a family-oriented faith that is passed on from parent to child, such as illustrated in the simple faith expressed in the life of young Timothy (2 Tim. 1:5).

This nurture-oriented faith would then mature to the point of acceptance of doctrines and beliefs which have provided the historical content of the person's community of faith. (See 1 Tim. 4:6.)

There is a further step of potential growth that depends on a Christian's ability to personalize his or her beliefs. This requires not only mastering the *content* of one's faith, but examining these beliefs in light of alternatives and personal experience. That is, the believer tests *what* he or she has come to believe against the realities of personal experience. Out of this encounter between *what* others have valued and one's personal conscience, develops convictions regarding the *why* and *how* of that person's faith. (See 1 Tim. 1:19.)

So faith is *what* I believe but it is also—at a more mature stage—*why* and *how* I believe (act/live). A growing faith conveys a pilgrim image, always seeking and trying, yet never achieving perfection in the likeness of Christ.

THE PHASES OF FAITH DEVELOPMENT

As I came to understand faith as an active, growing force, I began to search for the pattern of development in my life. After doing much reflection, I identified five rather distinct yet interwoven phases:

Nurture	(ages 0-6)
Indoctrination	(ages 7-18)
Reality Testing	(ages 19-27)
Making Choices	(ages 28-35)
Active Devotion	(ages 36-up)

NURTURE (through about age 6)

This was the primary exposure to and awareness of the meaning of life which I received from my family and church during early childhood. I came to feel love and security, and to understand that these persons wanted me to be like they were.

I remember that going to Sunday School and church services was very special, that we met in God's house, that I loved Jesus and he loved me, and that my family and home were Christian. If I misbehaved, I thought it made God mad—and that he could always see me no matter how hard I tried to hide.

My parents and my Sunday School teachers had the greatest influence on my life. I can't remember too much about *what* they taught me; but I do remember how much they cared for and loved me.

INDOCTRINATION (ages 7-18)

During these years, I recall seeking avidly to master the content of my faith. This content came from the Bible, curriculum materials, and what my parents, teachers, ministers, and other significant persons told me was true. I memorized much material, learned how to act as a Christian, discovered what I could and could not say at church, and otherwise formed the foundation for knowing and believing in an acceptable way as a Christian in my community of faith. Whereas in the early years I learned what authorities said was important (can you remember believing that if something was printed in a book or said by a teacher or preacher, that it was absolutely true?), during my teenage years I looked more to what other youth were doing, saying, and believing.

I was fortunate in that my closest peers were oriented toward evangelical Christianity. We went to school together, played together, and had many religious experiences in common. When I was a teenager, there was a great emphasis on Christian youth being good and having fun, with little emphasis on doctrinal issues and theological concerns. Consequently, I learned how to be good, thus was viewed as an outstanding Christian young person in my church.

At the age of twelve, I made a public profession of faith. I remember three distinct impressions during that time: (1) I knew it was the right time for me to confess my sins and give my life to Jesus; (2) I was concerned about how the preacher would baptize me so as to keep water from getting in my nose; and (3) I wanted to be able to take part in the Lord's Supper. These may be unusual things to recall, but as I know now, they are very typical of children who grow up in Christian homes. My conversion experience was a response to what was *right* and *expected* in my faith community. I had learned well how to be the best Christian I was capable of being at that point in my development.

Through the ensuing years I continued to learn what was acceptable, was at church every time the doors opened, and sought to pattern my life after the models I had chosen: C. Roy Angell, Pat Terrilli, John Rodgers, Ona Barfield, Ann Alexander, Betty and Fred Childers, and others. I learned how to be a successful Christian according to the standards of my faith community. This was indoctrination in the best sense.

As I remember those years, I look back with fondness and appreciation for what they gave me—both in content and in nurture. During the first phase, nurture was most important to me and to them. This care continued into the second phase, but they and I gradually focused more on mastering the content of my faith (what to believe and how to behave). This gave me the foundation on which I could begin my personal journey into knowing God. What was given were the best answers they had, and I learned them well. But as I began to discover toward the end of my teen years, their answers—which I had interpreted as literal forms, methods, and contents of *the* faith—were not always adequate in my experience.

Gradually, I began to recognize that much of my faith—my way of knowing God—was secondhand, and that their answers would not always work for me as I faced new people, places, and experiences. The way I had been taught to view God and my life was changing, and I didn't feel good about it. In fact, I felt downright guilty about even thinking that some of the answers I had believed might not fit new situations.

Thus, at about nineteen, I began to compare my perception of life with the faith system I had acquired from a congregation whose nurture, beliefs, ministry, and ongoing love I cherished and respected.

REALITY TESTING (ages 19-27)

During these years I ventured out into the larger world of places, ideas, and experiences. Rather than being located primarily in the familiar environment of my childhood—dependent on home, family, friends, and the authority-support of my faith community—I established my own home in another state. I took a new job, went to college, joined a church, and, in general, began a new phase of life. But I began this new phase with a set of values and beliefs with which my previous community had equipped me.

It did not take me long to discover that many things that had worked well for me previously no longer applied. Without thinking, I had begun a process of testing. As I recall, this began during high school years as I sought to establish an identity separate from that of my parents—making some of my own decisions, getting a part-time job so I could earn and spend my own money, dressing and behaving my way, and so on. Most of this early testing was not directly related to faith, however, because my faith concepts were so closely aligned with my peer group experience.

But the move from home, and subsequent self-dependence, created new situations in which I had to use the knowledge, attitudes, and skills learned earlier. Whenever I was successful, there was reinforcement that helped make these things *general principles* for my life. Whenever that which I knew, felt, or could do did not meet the need of a situation or created a problem for me, I was faced with either trying to make my previous answer fit by rationalizing the situation, or trying to relearn in light of new information.

I found that every dimension of my life came under scrutiny. So much of my religion, work habits, patterns of living, and even personal life-style previously had been community-oriented, first in my family and then in my peer group.

Gradually, I came to feel that whatever I was knowing, feeling, or doing had to be *mine*. That which I packed and carried with me from earlier years was my parents', my church's, my group's, or my culture's, and I became disillusioned as I saw parts of my past were inconsistent with present experience.

I recall vividly two experiences related to this phase. First, I recall on a visit home that I shared with my mother some of the new insights I had gained about the Bible. She replied with great concern, "You mustn't say things like that!" I was amused and disturbed at her response. She didn't change my mind, but I did learn to keep most of my new ideas to myself.

The other experience was related to general outlook on life. I had developed a belief that people love each other and have basic commitments to justice and honesty. Although this was the pattern in my protected world of childhood and teenage years, I became keenly disappointed as I found that this belief was not always correct.

In this phase, I moved from high idealism—feeling that my newfound answers were the answers for all time and all places— to a realistic appraisal of a life in which what one knows, feels, and does must be consistent with life experiences.

MAKING CHOICES (ages 28-35)

This period of life came into focus as I gradually acknowledged that whatever choices were made to direct my life must be mine, and that every choice would have consequences with which I would have to live.

Whereas the time of reality testing surfaced the inconsistencies between my present experiences and the answers which were passed to me by my home, church, and culture, now I had to resolve these questions.

As I recall those years, there were two very distinct urges—or pulls—during the transition that led to this phase. The first urge

I felt was to reach out and grab many of the new ideas and ways of doing things which promised easy answers, even radical answers, to my questions.

The second feeling came a bit later, probably in response to my easy acceptance of some answers which were quite different from those of my childhood. This urge was the opposite of the first: to grasp the answers I had always known and to hold very tightly. I was struggling to meet a very basic human need, *security*. I was uncomfortable in the tension of not knowing exactly what, why, when, and how about my faith, my church life, my vocation, my family, and my future.

The growth point for me was when I realized how both these pulls were working on me, that they existed side by side, and that they were a *natural* part of the maturing process. The question for me was: Do I succumb to *either* pull? Each was an answer, an easy answer. But I realized that both represented viewpoints held and decisions made by others. *They were not mine.* I would have to accept the tension—the pulls from these two influences—and begin to make *my* choices.

This decision led to the first testing point. When I made choices, I had to take the consequences. No longer could I disappear into the crowd and let the group, the movement, my age, place in life, parents, church, or culture take responsibility for me. Decisions were mine and I had to take the results—good or bad. There was no blaming others.

For me, this was another conversion experience. My initial affirmation of faith was an act of accepting that to which I had been exposed. During this period of life my commitment was an act of consciously choosing from a variety of alternatives, many of them quite impressive. Whereas my earlier decision was more *when* to affirm publicly my identity as a Christian, this experience focused on choosing what, how, and why I would believe and live. The reaction from significant others to my earlier experience was predictably supportive, and my life went on as usual. The reaction from others during this phase, however, was not so predictable nor could life proceed as if nothing had happened. Decisions led to life changes, which produced consequences for which I had to assume responsibility.

This process of developing, testing, and clarifying personal choices continued to be the major task of my faith development well into my middle thirties. If I could have done this alone, it would have been a simpler process. But every choice influenced other choices, and consequences for my decisions ultimately had to be considered in a context of how they affected others in my family, social group, church, community, and work. Also, one person does not walk this path alone; we are all on a similar faith pilgrimage. We choose, develop, test, and clarify choices in an intergenerational community of persons, all of whom are somewhere on this path.

ACTIVE DEVOTION (age 36 and up)

Growing out of the pressures experienced during earlier phases, my concerns began to shift during my latter thirties to the ways in which I could most effectively live my convictions. Not that all of the struggles and searching done in earlier stages was left behind, but rather there seemed to be a sense of satisfaction coming from having worked through many issues, along with a heightened need to express this faith in everyday life. The urgency shifted from making choices to living and propagating my faith.

In *Christian Leadership* I told of my struggles to clarify the ways in which a Christian may legitimately seek to guide others. Much of the searching described was characteristic of the previous phase. As I moved into this period, however, my major concerns began to focus on ways I must practice in every part of my life the principles to which I had committed myself. I felt compelled to live this style of leadership as well as seek to be an evangelist for it.

I no longer feel as defensive about my beliefs as I did in earlier phases. I guess this comes from having consciously made my faith my own through examining options, looking at consequences, and testing it out in the day-to-day realities of life. I have the conviction that it is my own, that it is right for me, and by growing through to this point I know how to examine and renew it as situations change. So I have no need to defend my faith from the close examination of others, nor do I hesitate to share it as something that has been a life-changing experience for me.

But I also recognize that my pilgrimage has been rather unique. No one else has walked the path exactly like I have. Consequently, I have become much more open to the views of others and tolerant of persons expressing their Christian commitments in different ways. This has been apparent as I find myself desiring fellowship with and able better to understand and accept the faith expressions of persons who are at different phases than I.

OBSERVATIONS

As I look back, there are some key points which have helped me in understanding my spiritual growth. Let me share them with you simply as personal observations.

(1) Each phase represents a developmental task that is dominant at a particular point in life. They are sequential, and one has to master (or complete) each one before the next step becomes important.

(2) All phases are interrelated. Faith development cannot be divided into compartments. Rather it can be likened to the growth of a plant: seed, root, stem, leaf, bud, bloom. Each step happens in sequence, yet all are dependent on the earlier and continuing phases. All phases are the plant; the bloom is no more the plant than are the leaves or roots. So it is with faith; all phases *are* faith. Yet there is a distinct pattern of development.

(3) There is a movement from known to unknown, concrete to abstract, certain to uncertain. As a child, all I knew about faith was from direct experience—there was no concept of the

unknown. I was told answers and accepted them; doubt existed only until an authority (person, book, rule, etc.) could speak. In later years, however, I was faced with the discrepancies, the unknowns, the elements of mystery in my religion. Rather than ignore these unknowns, I reworked my faith according to the way I viewed life.

(4) One's capacity to face and openly accept inconsistencies in his or her beliefs while demonstrating active devotion can be a sign of a deep and secure faith. The movement from known to unknown and certainty to uncertainty requires enlarged dimensions of faith. That which can be explained, and is sure and absolute according to human standards, requires little capacity for faith. Verification is always possible by consulting appropriate authorities. Conversely, to accept that which cannot be proved or explained requires an enlarged faith.

(5) The authority for decision-making gradually changes. During the early phases parents and then teachers, pastors, and other authority figures are the ultimate decision makers and determiners of right and wrong. Then a peer group becomes the judge. As faith continues to grow, the responsibility for decision-making moves to each individual. At this point, persons must test their way of believing and decide why, where, and how authority will be exercised in their lives.

(6) Each phase follows a predictable pattern, beginning with a gradual resolution of issues and conflicts which started the change. This transition evolves into a time of relative comfort and security. The major questions have been answered, and there is a predictable pattern for expressing one's faith in an acceptable way. A phase ends when changes within or without begin to create problems which cannot be resolved easily in the manner of believing or acting learned during that particular phase. Thus, potential is created for growth to a new phase.

(7) The basic needs for growth and for security are continuing forces which may help or hinder movement from phase to phase. Growth comes as a person successfully resolves the issues and

conflicts that occur during the transition between phases. On the other hand, the tension that arises upon facing conflict at the end of a phase can be painful, causing a person to retreat to the security of that which has been known and experienced. There is potential for growth and for security in each phase, and these dual urges produce an approach-avoidance, or ambivalent feeling.

(8) Growth is achieved at a cost. Resolving tensions and questions in life takes not only work but also requires that persons overcome the human desire for comfort, security, and predictability. If a balance between these dual attractions cannot be achieved, security needs can block any natural opportunities for growth.

(9) Security can be a by-product of a growing faith. Whereas security in the early phases of faith development is found in *what* one believes and does, continuing growth yields security of a different nature. Rather than seeking the known, predictable forms of authority, answers, and practices, there is a by-product of security in the *why* and *how* one believes and lives. Instead of finding security in *possessing* the faith, there seems to be a sense of comfort derived from being in a continual process of *maturing* in faith. One's trust is in a faithful and growing relationship with God that can best be expressed according to purpose and principles that guide a believer's life. Security comes not in having and holding as much as in seeking and finding.

(10) One primary outcome of a growing faith is active Christian service. Personal convictions lead to commitments, which are expressed in Christian service. That which results from a more mature faith is done out of a sense of personal desire. It is not dependent on others; rather it is initiated, motivated, and reinforced mainly through one's personal relationship with God.

Christian service may be a part of earlier phases; however, for me it was done primarily out of a sense of oughtness, or because I felt it was my responsibility or duty. At that time, service was more of a learned response to a particular situation or need (the *what* of Christian faith). For example, in my early years as a Christian I thought the only way to witness was to approach a stranger and tell him or her what the Bible says about Jesus. Now I view witnessing in a much broader way—as a natural part of what I want to share with anyone, anywhere.

(11) The other major outcome of a growing faith is acceptance of the ways in which you are maturing, and tolerance (understanding) of others who may be experiencing faith development in a different way. Every person has direct access to God and to the Scriptures, and each tests his or her understandings and commitments in light of personal differences. As one matures in the faith, these differences in interpretation become less of a test for faithfulness than expressions of love, mercy, justice, and service on behalf of God and in witness to one's Lord.

Continual growth—involving testing, refining, and developing the best ways of living out one's Christian convictions—becomes an expected part of life. Rather than protesting or defending what has been, or allowing religion to become creedal or ritualistic, intentional effort is devoted to seeking out and discovering effective ways of doing God's will.

LEARNING ACTIVITIES

1. How do you respond to this statement?
   Faith is an *interpretation* of the way persons have experienced life. Rather than being something we believe that can be compiled, taught, and tested, it is a *way* of knowing the unknowable.
2. Using the following outline, list some of the memorable experiences in your faith development. If you are studying this with others, share these experiences and tell how they relate to the phases described in this chapter.
   Nurture—

   Indoctrination—

Reality Testing—

Making Choices—

Active Devotion—

3. Describe where you are now in your spiritual growth.

_____

_____

_____

_____

_____

_____

_____

Discuss this with others if you wish. This will also be used for reference in later learning activities.

2
How Faith Grows

At age nine I became a Christian and joined the church. I was influenced largely by my parents and by my pastor so my faith was basically the faith of my parents and pastor.

At age fourteen during the teenage years, I began assuming more responsibility for my personal commitments and beliefs. College years through age twenty-four—basically I held the basic beliefs of my church community. (I remember being defensive about my faith.)

About age thirty I gained an increased awareness of values of truth in other positions other than my own. This is where I find myself now.

> School teacher; age 38
> Rural background

Faith is such a nebulous thing. And yet it is there; it begins, and grows, and changes. How do you get a handle on this process beyond that which happens to *you*? How does a person develop the assurance of things hoped for and the conviction of things not seen, as faith is illustrated in Hebrews 11:1?

AN INDIVIDUAL PERSPECTIVE

It is no more possible to live without faith than to live without eating. Faith in the broadest sense is an indispensable ingredient developed from birth. As an individual learns by experience how best to relate to his or her environment, deep impressions develop such as the predictable elements in nature, the ways in which certain actions cause predictable results, and the degree of trust one can have in certain people.

These beliefs gradually are refined as individuals consciously test and refine their perception of the trustworthiness, or predictableness, of the *what* or *who* in the faith relationship. The process would proceed through a continuing cycle as in figure 1.

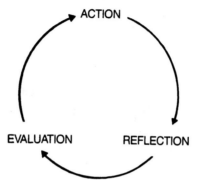

Figure 1

ACTION

Although a person might enter the cycle at any point, the usual beginning is with personal experience, or *action*. Here, one interacts with the people and circumstances of his or her environment.

In this continuing series of interactions, the individual receives a flow of messages which must be interpreted and used in coping with the source of these influences.

REFLECTION

Reflection is the feeling and thinking response which follows personal experience. This activity may be very short, as in the case of an action-response sequence that has become extremely predictable (example: smile in response to a smile), or rather involved (example: wondering why a friend is unhappy).

This activity generally determines the amount of effort you will put into making an adjustment in your response to those people or circumstances. Usually, more attention will be given to actions that will decrease pain (dissatisfaction) and/or increase pleasure (satisfaction).

EVALUATION

If change is deemed necessary, this step requires an assessment of options and potential consequences. The key question is: How best can I adjust my actions to alleviate the pain or increase the pleasure?

This step focuses on changes one must make in order to cope successfully with the situation as perceived through personal experience.

Thus, any steps deemed necessary are taken so as to relate in an appropriate way to outside influences, and the cycle goes on: action, reflection, and evaluation. This same process applies to all dimensions of faith development: *Knowing* (the content of my faith), and *doing* (the works of my faith).

A COMMUNITY PERSPECTIVE

Perhaps a more inclusive description of the faith development process comes from a community perspective. For faith ultimately resides in, is nurtured by, and finds greatest expression within a body of like-minded believers. Not that persons and situations not a part of the body lack influence; rather the initiative and reinforcement that ultimately count reside among a significant people and tradition to which the individual gives allegiance.

The individual perspective described above operates *within* the community context. As I initially described in *Christian Leadership*, this approach must be seen as *individual and corporate*. Despite the personal nature of the struggle for discovery, development, and fulfillment, this very process is dependent on the dominant influences of a loving, supportive community of faith which will nurture and support the growth process. Let me illustrate how faith might grow in a Christian community.[1]

The environment most conducive to growth is one permeated with purpose when every action, every structure, every decision reflects the reason for being. There exists in such a community a high degree of congruence between surface characteristics and the essence of the organization.

Koinonia, a Greek word used in the New Testament to describe the church, gives us an idea of what Christians might expect if they earnestly seek to understand and follow God's will. Oneness, unity, caring, sharing, and supportive fellowship are all descriptive of *koinonia,* yet they don't quite capture the gist implied in the New Testament. Really, the word *koinonia* suggests that all of these things are possible, but only because of the presence of something greater than that which the people involved might represent.

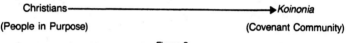

Christians ──────────────────────────► *Koinonia*
(People in Purpose)   (Covenant Community)

Figure 2

In this diagram, the direction of Christian growth is indicated: toward a type of community such as that implied by the word *koinonia.* As indicated on the left, Christians have a common Lord and common purpose—thus the term, People in Purpose. However, they are one in the Spirit only because of their relationship to Jesus Christ; there is no automatic caring, sharing, supportive fellowship among strangers. Only as they become a community of believers and develop an environment of *koinonia* can Christians understand and appreciate what it means to be the body of Christ (see Col. 1:18).

Assuming that moving toward *koinonia* is an acceptable direction of Christian growth, how does it happen? How can you recognize it? And how can you encourage it?

We are prone to assume that such a relationship develops automatically, that it is simply a by-product of Christian people being together. But, upon reflection, few of us would try to explain this so glibly.

In trying to understand how *koinonia* develops, let's look at another diagram.

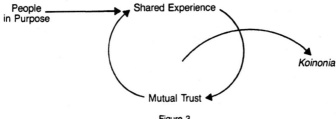

Figure 3

As Christians (People in Purpose) come together, they share many things—study, worship, fellowship, and such. Then an interesting thing happens. As people share experiences together, mutual trust and faith in each other begin to develop. Let me give you an example.

In establishing a friendship you usually have initial experiences such as introductions, handshaking, and small talk. These limited experiences provide an initial exposure which, in a very small way, breaks down barriers between people. This interaction, if satisfying, elicits a slight amount of trust and acceptance between those involved. And more shared experience creates potential for more mutual trust. Thus the friendship intensifies until one person in the relationship ceases to match the other, either in experiences shared or in level of trust. Then the friendship tends to stabilize at that level.

Now let's look at the church. As experiences are shared, people develop a little bit of faith and trust in each other. This creates a potential for more shared experiences. And, as in developing a friendship, the cycle progresses as people experience more things together and gain a greater degree of mutual trust. The difference here is that the growth cycle can continue even if some individuals drop out along the way (as is the case in any congregation). But here is the key: As Christians grow in shared experience and mutual trust, they also are maturing in their faith; this is because who they are and what they do is a reflection of their purpose for being together.

It is some time during this maturing process that Christians begin to become aware of something that cannot be explained in human terms—*koinonia*. Through the gift of God, Christians find themselves in a growing relationship which in the eyes of the world defies explanation. They become a caring, sharing, supportive group of Christians who can do all things through Christ that build his church.

Relating this to a church we as teachers and leaders cannot give people purpose; that is something that comes as a person accepts Jesus Christ as Lord and Savior. Nor can we create and give people *koinonia*—that is a gift from God. But what we can do is encourage and enable Christians to create the potential for *koinonia*—to pursue growth individually and as a body, praying that God will guide and strengthen them as they seek to be his people. Then God in his wisdom will empower and bless to accomplish his purpose.

AN INTEGRATED PERSPECTIVE: INDIVIDUAL AND COMMUNITY

Over the years I have come to appreciate qualities in some people that seem to enable them to learn from a great variety of experiences—be they good or bad. These people have an outlook on life that transcends the ordinary. Apparently not hampered by a fear of failure and not controlled by a desire for success, they value every experience simply because they are able to learn about themselves and about their world. As they reflect on and react to various situations in life, they grow.

This does not mean that a person floats about, pushed by every wave; rather in all experiences both intended and coincidental— one is able to find meaning that enables one to become a more complete or more mature individual. Christians, indeed, are urged to "Rejoice always, pray constantly, give thanks in all circumstances; for this is the will of God in Christ Jesus for you" (1 Thess. 5:16-18, RSV). But what qualities enable a person to hold such an outlook on life?

I was helped in identifying these qualities while attending a marriage enrichment retreat led by author-teacher Reuel Howe. He described his struggle to understand the direction of growth and how various personal and community factors influence the extent and the meaning of all experiences. Let me describe some of his insights and the ideas he spawned in my mind.

Illustrated is a lifeline. It begins on the left at the point of conception and continues to the right, not toward death but toward life—or toward full maturity in Jesus Christ.

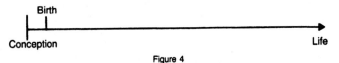

Figure 4

While in the womb, the fetus is comfortable and secure, growing toward independence from the mother's body. At birth, the infant enters the world to new experiences and for the first time must begin to seek satisfaction for basic needs.

The young child is usually fortunate and has great success in meeting his needs. He learns to wiggle, to crawl, to walk, to run, to cry, to babble, to speak words, and, later, sentences. In essence, he begins to master his world, partly because of those who care for him and partly due to maturation. And so life develops.

But a strange thing begins to happen to the child and to the youth and to the young adult. Those built-in, protected chances for successful growth and development occur less and less frequently. And the potential for failure—and consequent pain—increases inversely.

Whereas a child will learn to walk, to talk, and to control his bowel movements, there are no such future guarantees as a person gradually moves into a life in which success is not assured. During this transition a person comes to see that in every new experience the potential for pain is as real as for pleasure. Thus, as a part of this process, the qualities begin to emerge that determine one's approach to growing faith.

As a person becomes involved in new experiences, one seeks success (pleasure) and avoids failure (pain). When young, due to a predominance of success, a child ventures into many new experiences. But one becomes wary of pain, and as one grows older, one becomes wiser; that is, he avoids doing things that might lead to failure.

Here, then, particularly as a person leaves school, settles down, and escapes the demands of having to face new experiences, comes the point of escape. Rather than continue growing toward life—and risking pain as well as pleasure—some people retreat to a womb-like existence. By risking little in terms of new experiences, they feel secure—like a fetus in its mother.

But such a life-style not only restricts a growing faith, it also assures that a person cannot fulfill the biblical expectation that Christians are to worship, to witness, to minister, and to teach, regardless of the consequences.

Now, I am not suggesting that Christians who want to keep growing lack feeling; that they can experience failure but not hurt. This just isn't so. However, the process of growth must be viewed as shown in figure 5, where the growth toward greater maturity is more a series of advances and retreats, successes and failures, pleasure and pain. Always, the risk of growth is faced not just for the success that might be achieved but for the value that accrues in trying to become all that one is capable of becoming as a child of God.

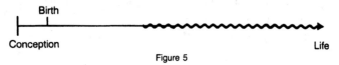

Figure 5

Thus, success is desirable but not necessary, and failure is always a possibility. The value is in the growth that occurs, regardless of the outcome. And the direction of personal experience, though it may have setbacks, is always toward a fuller and more mature expression of the Christian life.

The personal qualities that evolve in this process may be viewed as characteristics a person exhibits when moving either toward life or toward the "womb." Here are some easily observed examples:

Toward Womb	Personal Characteristics	Toward Life
Closed stance		Open stance
Opaque self		Transparent self
Other controlled		Self-controlled
Past/Future oriented		Present oriented
Preserving		Transforming
Over-rational		Emotionally honest
Formal education		Lifelong learning
"Ought" commitment		"Want" commitment

Figure 6

The person moving toward life will, in general, value and exemplify the characteristics listed on the right. This does not mean the person has achieved or will ever achieve the end represented by the characteristics. But the progression generally is away from the womb-type traits toward the qualities listed under *life*. This is a journey, with successes and failures, advances and retreats, attempted to achieve a fuller expression of Christian maturity.

Let me describe in very broad terms how a growing Christian might view these issues.

Open stance *vs.* Closed stance—This refers primarily to outlook on life. The life-seeking person tends to be open to new experiences, ideas, and directions; a tryer, one who values continual growth.

Transparent self *vs.* Opaque self—The honest, real self is very important to the life-seeker. Little energy is expended in maintaining a role or a facade. This does not mean a person is tactless or crude, rather one has a healthy self-concept and feels one can love and be loved as one is.

Self-controlled *vs.* Other-controlled—This relates not to self-sufficiency, for the life-seeking person is extremely dependent on others, but to the motivation in one's life. When a facade is necessary and a person cannot be oneself, control by others is strong. The life-seeking person responds to an inner motivation and acts by choice based on personal commitments.

Present-oriented *vs.* Past/Future-oriented—Rather than treasuring the good old days or living for the future, this quality relates to the activity of a person as one is and where one is now; there is no escape to another time or place. For the life-seeker, the past is a servant of the present—providing valuable insights into understanding and coping with present experience—and the future will be a child of the present. What happens now is life; all that was or will be, if dwelled upon, becomes an escape from reality.

Transforming *vs.* Preserving—Here, again, the emphasis is not on a choice between transforming or preserving. Rather the decision must be made in terms of priority: are we to focus most of our resources on receiving, conserving, and preserving everything that exists; or are we to evaluate what exists and, based on our commitments, seek to transform that which may not be acceptable. Perhaps the best example of this is given by David Hunter in *Christian Education as Engagement:* Are we called to preserve our culture as we receive it, or do we seek to transform it in light of Christian beliefs?

Emotionally honest *vs.* Overly rational—The life-seeking person responds to head and to heart, to reasoning and to feeling. Both responses, as long as they are honest, represent variables that significantly influence life, and thus learning and growing. There is little effort made to rationalize or to explain away feelings or actions which may be based on feelings. An honest want or desire does not have to be explained rationally. It simply exists.

Lifelong learning *vs.* Formal education—Every experience can be an opportunity for learning. A person need not depend solely on the systematic, graded approach to education generally offered in a classroom. Reflection on spontaneous or unstructured activities and feelings, informal inquiry growing out of personal interest, and problem solving through trial and error are some of the opportunities for growth that are available throughout life. Obviously we all continue learning regardless of our orientation in this area. But the life-seeking person generally perceives all experience as opportunity for learning and growing; thus one's expectations often enable one to gain or improve knowledge, attitudes, and skills when others may perceive nothing of value. Thus it is fairly evident that the life seeker places great value on the process of learning instead of simply stressing the study of subjects.

The life seeker does not reject the content of formalized education. Rather one uses it in service to the present and in preparation for the future. Added to content however must be a process of learning where the development of problem-solving skills and of personal values is dominant. Using education in achieving a satisfying and meaningful life under any combination of circumstances is the desired goal.

"Want" commitment *vs.* "Ought" commitment—This characteristic grows out of a basic tension in every person between developing one's own values and accepting the values of others, for their incorporation is primarily due to the permeating influence of significant persons experienced since birth. The tension begins when a person begins to examine these passed-down values in light of his present experience and finds discrepancies. At this point the person can either avoid reality and seek to reinforce presently-held values, or one can begin the process of adjusting his value system so that it is congruent with one's experience.

Basically, the life-seeking person feels free to evaluate and make one's own commitments; one tends to avoid operating out of "oughtness" which indicates that one is controlled by outside forces.

As a Christian, the life seeker is one who has consciously struggled with and developed personal convictions concerning one's relationship to Jesus Christ. Rather than accepting religious convictions secondhand or simply affirming parental commitments, one appraises one's world and comes up with values and beliefs for which one can stand without being motivated by guilt feelings.

These are some of the features that create the image of a growing person, one committed to seeking an ever-increasing maturity in Jesus Christ.

No one feature stands alone; all are interconnected, and success or failure in one area affects the others. Even so, the basic expectation of life-seeking persons is that the overall direction of personal and spiritual growth is toward life and away from a sequestered or dormant existence.

RELATIONSHIP BETWEEN ENVIRONMENT AND PERSONAL QUALITIES

The relationship between the environment in which one lives and personal qualities that are developed is something like the proverbial question about which came first, the chicken or the egg. One's environment is the greatest influence on the development of life-seeking qualities. But it is a commitment to life-seeking values by a community of people that creates such an environment.

As a person practices life-seeking behavior, it is the response of persons who are significant to one that either encourages or discourages similar actions in the future. For example, if a person tries something and fails, there is a great deal of difference between a supportive, encouraging environment and one that conveys an I-told-you-so reaction.

The environment or community that values trying encourages

life-seeking behavior. When a person succeeds there is not only praise and recognition but also support and encouragement for continued growth. The general pattern is not so much to recognize success as an end in itself; rather success is valued as a stepping-stone in the growth process toward spiritual maturity.

When success is incomplete or failure occurs, the environmental support and encouragement increases rather than diminishes, and the community helps those who are involved focus on reflection. This is for the purpose of examining feelings, understanding motives, evaluating actions, and determining the learning gained simply because of being involved in the experience.

Thus both the content of learning and the process through which one acquires that content provide opportunities for growth. And it is the environment in which people live that develops within them a grow or no-grow attitude toward these opportunities.

LEARNING ACTIVITIES

1. Describe your conversion experience. How and when did you decide that you had become a different person?

   _____

   _____

   _____

2. Using the information that describes figure 1, explain *how* you came to conversion.

   A. What was your life like before becoming a Christian?

   _____

   B. What did you think about your life and the future?

   _____

   C. How did you decide that Christ is the best answer?

   _____

   _____

3. Explain the most important contribution your church or group makes to your spiritual growth. What personal qualities have you developed as a result of this influence? _____

_____

_____

3
Understanding Your Faith

When I was a child, I spoke like a child, I thought like a child. . . . When I became a man, I gave up childish ways. For now we see in a mirror dimly, but then face to face. Now I know in part; then shall I understand fully, even as I have been fully understood (1 Cor. 13:11-12, RSV).

Evangelist; middle-aged
Jewish background

Faith, as has been described, is a unique personal response of belief and trust to the revelation which has been received through a community of believers. Implicit in this response is the notion that one does not enter the faith relationship with God and his people as a fully developed believer. Rather, regardless of age, one begins the maturing process as a babe—one newborn in the faith. And the growth which follows is part of discipleship development—in the image of a pilgrim striving toward a life in the likeness of one's Lord.

If faith development does indeed proceed from a limited expression toward maturity, it follows that we can examine our own lives and learn something of how we have fared in the growth process. Indeed, by careful examination of the development of a great many persons, we can begin to give clearer definition to the process itself—what happens and when.

Efforts have been in progress to identify the phases of human development for many years; and much has been learned by the average person about the passages or stages through which one moves. It was during the latter 1970s, however, that this attention focused more narrowly on the way humans experience faith development.

I have described for you my faith pilgrimage, given you a chance to describe yours, and have suggested how faith grows. The next step for us is to see what we can learn from the actual experiences of others so that we can have a basis for comparison, evaluation, and understanding. This is not to give us the answers; rather it is to describe the usual pattern of faith development as determined from studies of a large number of people.

To illustrate current thinking, I want to share with you the interpretations which two prominent writers give to faith development.

RINGS OF A TREE

One of the clearest descriptions comes in the form of a visual impression: Faith grows like the rings of a tree, with each ring adding to and changing the tree somewhat, yet building on that which has grown before.

John H. Westerhoff, a professor at Duke University Divinity School, suggests the tree analogy and proposes four rings which are involved in the growth process.[1]

EXPERIENCED FAITH

As illustrated in figure 7, at the core is the faith which we experience from our earliest years either in life or, if one has a major reorientation in his or her beliefs, in a new faith system. We receive the faith that is important to those who nurture us. The way it molds and influences their lives makes an indelible impression on us, creating the core of our faith. It is by this initial experience in the way of knowing and responding to people and situations that persons begin to develop their faith impressions and values.

This level of faith is usually associated with the impressionable

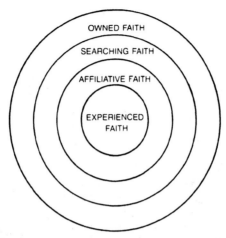

Figure 7

periods of life when a person is dependent on others, such as during early childhood.

AFFILIATIVE FAITH

As a person gradually displays the beliefs, values, and practices of one's family, group, or church, there is another ring formed. The individual takes on the characteristics of the nurturing persons and becomes identified as an accepted partner, one who is part of the faith tradition. Such participation may be formalized as in membership, a rite of baptism or confirmation, or may simply be understood, as might be the case with regular participants who do not join a church.

This phase of a person's growth is recognized as a time of testing. It is a matching of the person with peer expectations. Where traditions, values, and practices are similar, there usually is a good match and the individual merges his or her identity with that of the body. There is little room for personal differences due to a strong emphasis on unity and conformity in belief and practice.

Persons who do not have a good match at this time in their pilgrimage must seek other situations, or find persons more sensitive to meeting the needs which exist. The concerns for belonging, for security, and for a sense of power (and identity) that come from group membership are the key drives in forming one's faith concepts during this period.

This level of faith usually is expressed, at the earliest, during adolescent years. It may also be apparent in a person's life whenever there is a need such as for security, right answers, improved morals, or clear identity regarding who one is or what one believes.

SEARCHING FAITH

Faith development reaches a crucial junction when one becomes aware that personal beliefs or experience may no longer be exactly the same as those of the group, or when a person begins to question some of the commonly held beliefs or practices. This occurs as one naturally recognizes that his or her faith is formed more by others (parents, peers, congregation, etc.) than by personal conviction.

The decision must be faced whether or not to develop, express, and accept responsibility for a *personal* interpretation of one's religion as over against accepting that which may be viewed as the group's interpretation. This involves a reorientation in an individual's view of how God relates to his people, primarily at the point of responsibility. As a person begins to move into this phase the concern is: To what degree must I accept responsibility for my own relationship with God and for the ways in which I express this in my daily life?

At the same time that this natural desire to search for one's own commitments arises, there is an opposite force that urges persons to hold fast to the known, the experienced, the commonly held expressions of faith. This urge also is very natural, representing a basic human need for security, acceptance, and simplicity.

Those who progress into this phase must inevitably question the content and expressions characteristic of the affiliative faith level. There is an examination of alternatives, looking logically at the traditions, values, and teachings from a variety of perspectives. Often there is experimentation in which persons try out alternatives or commit themselves to persons or causes which promise help in establishing personal convictions and active practice of one's faith.

Such is the struggle characteristic of this phase, yet it is the way that people must pass in order to make personal commitments, deepen convictions, and prepare themselves for actively expressing and accepting responsibility for their faith.

OWNED FAITH

The culmination of the faith development process finds expression in a personal, owned faith. This best could be described as a conversion experience, in which a person has reoriented his or her life and now claims personal ownership of and responsibility for beliefs and practices.

The struggles and searching associated with the previous phase do not disappear entirely but are resolved in a trusting acceptance that the commitments made are a faithful response to the call of God. Thus one can then freely choose to claim to be a disciple, identifying with like-minded persons who also have chosen to follow the same beliefs and practices.

Characteristics of this phase include close attention to practicing one's faith as well as believing it; increased attention to active involvement in in-depth Bible study, prayer/devotional/meditation experiences, and personal mission/ministry efforts; and a natural life-style of sharing with others the value of one's faith.

This level of faith, according to Westerhoff, is God's intention for everyone; we all are called to reach our highest potential. However, all expressions of faith are in response to the nurture of God's Spirit and his people, thus must be acknowledged as a faithful though perhaps not ideal response to the ever-seeking, ever-calling Word.[2]

STAGES OF FAITH

A more detailed description of spiritual formation has been proposed by James W. Fowler. Growing out of a research project involving interviews with about four hundred persons, he has identified six stages which encompass the faith development process from birth through maturity.[3]

STAGE 1—INTUITIVE-PROJECTIVE FAITH

In this foundational stage, one's faith is highly oriented toward the examples and expressions of parents and other significant adults. Usually associated with early childhood, this faith involves much imitation and fantasy, reflective of the powerful influences exerted by others through their examples, moods, actions, and language.

STAGE 2—MYTHIC-LITERAL FAITH

At this point, a person begins to take part in and adopt for oneself the stories, beliefs, and observances which are a part of one's faith community. The attitudes, beliefs, and practices are absorbed through informal exposure as well as through intentional, structured experiences. Learning focuses on literal interpretations, with distinct rules for judging right and wrong, good and bad, acceptable and unacceptable.

This faith holds to the beliefs and practices of a particular group or body. It provides security and is a cohesive force in the community. Authority and tradition during this stage are stronger influences on individuals than the desire for peer approval; and conformity is viewed as a virtue.

STAGE 3—SYNTHETIC-CONVENTIONAL FAITH

In this stage, a person's experience extends beyond the family and others who have been in the close-knit group of significant, caring persons. There exists a number of important areas of life such as family, work, school, peer group, leisure, community, and church. Out of this pattern of relationships and experiences the person in this stage adjusts his or her faith so tł t it ties life together. A *synthesis* of the common elements in one's pattern of relationships and experiences is developed; this is the way of *knowing*.

Since this faith is a reflection of the various parts of a person's environment and society, it is best described as *conventional*.

Beliefs and practices of this stage are determined largely either by authority figures, such as preachers or teachers, or by persons or groups considered significant or important, such as one's primary social group. It is these persons and groups who give form and structure to the various elements of life; consequently, persons are able to clarify the relationships and the meaning of faith. Such answers, however, are *adopted* from others; individuals at this level do not create their own responses to the meaning of life and faith.

STAGE 4—INDIVIDUATIVE-REFLECTIVE FAITH

The distinguishing characteristic of this stage is that a person assumes responsibility for his or her own commitments, taking whatever steps may be necessary to *individualize* the previously held conventional faith. This involves some element of risk, in that one must at least tentatively admit that the dominant expression of community faith is not sufficiently in accord with the world as he or she has come to view it.

When there has been a genuine transition to this stage, there is an open and honest struggle related to the *polar tensions* which have become apparent in one's life. One is experiencing pulls in both directions concerning issues such as:

Being an individual *vs.* Belonging to a group/community
Truth as I view it   *vs.* Truth as it is given to me
Self-fulfillment   *vs.* Service to others

Relative nature of   *vs.* Absolute nature of rules/laws
rules/laws

These issues can best be described as *personal* understanding
and commitment vs. *conventional* understanding and commitment.[4]

In the face of these uncomfortable feelings, there is a natural,
reflexive response: make a decision and solve the problem.
Fowler refers to this as the tendency toward *polar collapse*—to
settle for one set of answers based on either personal concerns or
on community pressures. This is an extreme position, sometimes
alienating a person from the self one has known, or from his or
her roots in the faith. Some persons illustrate this by rejecting
others who do not hold the same beliefs or practices to which
they have become committed.

Whereas identification with others in one's group was characteristic of the previous stage, self-chosen allegiance is given in
this phase not only to people but to rules and ideologies that
underlie groups or institutions. Concern with group boundaries
is typical, and patterns considered ideal for living, working, and
playing frequently are used to criticize the more conventional
approaches used by outsiders.[5]

Stage 4 presents a new and necessary kind of self-awareness.
Faith is caught in a cross-pull between expressions which are
conventional and other-directed, and those which are individu-
alized, self-chosen, and directed. Along with the necessity of
self-choice is a corresponding acceptance of responsibility for the
decisions which one makes.

STAGE 5—CONJUNCTIVE FAITH

Whereas in the previous stage there was a recognition of the
cross pulls in one's life, priority was given to the pull that exerted
the greater force. Decisions were made with an awareness of
what was being excluded as well as the consequences involved.
Once made, commitments led to efforts to reinforce and protect
personal positions even at the expense of degrading or attacking

positions held by other persons, institutions, or faith traditions.

In the transition from stage 4 to stage 5, the wrong seen in beliefs which do not agree with self-chosen viewpoints becomes less important. There comes a recognition that personal choices have been so emphasized that the integrity and truth which may be a part of other positions has been ignored.

Faith in this stage is expanded in the sense that

> it recognizes the integrity and truth in positions other than its own, and it affirms and lives out its own commitments and beliefs in such a way as to honor that which is true in the lives of others without denying the truth of its own. Stage 5 is ready for community of identification beyond tribal, racial, class, or ideological boundaries. *To be genuine, it must know the cost of such community and be prepared to pay the cost.* A true Stage 5 requires time and testing and regard for those who are different and who oppose you which Stage 4 does not have.[6]

The polar tensions experienced (and tentatively resolved) in the previous stage, resurface now not as issues which can be answered but as paradoxes that must exist. There is the possibility of truth and integrity in alternative positions as well as in the self-chosen ones. Time, place, and circumstance wield great influence over the perception of the correctness of a decision or action. Such is the nature of a paradoxical faith.

Yet, in many ways, this growth step enables one to consolidate his or her faith concepts. Rather than seeking to explain and master various parts of belief and practice, there comes a recognition of the limits of self-determination and a sense of acceptance of the great opposites in life, with a greater reliance on the source of all creation.

God can be accepted as personal *and* abstract, friend *and* judge, part of *and* apart from creation, unchanging *and* everchanging, Spirit *and* man. Jesus can be accepted as Master *and* Servant, past *and* present, divine *and* human. And humankind can be accepted as good *and* evil; community *and* individual, universal *and* local, finite *and* eternal, totally good in the likeness of God *and* good and depraved in the likeness of Adam.

Stage 5, according to Fowler, is the point at which faith comes to grips with the tensions of being ethically responsible yet finite. One must remain committed to practicing his or her faith regardless of the consequences, even while accepting the realities of ignorance, self-centeredness, and limited skills and motivation in oneself and in human kind generally.[7]

STAGE 6—UNIVERSALIZING FAITH

Building on all that has gone before, this stage embodies the kingdom of God as a live, felt reality for the person of faith. There is a sense of oneness a person has with the Creator and Sustainer as he or she participates in the work and worship rhythm of life.

There is an ability to transcend the human elements of physical, social, and personal concerns to focus on the broader issues of truth, justice, and goodness. One dwells in the world as a transforming presence but is not *of,* or controlled by the world.

No longer is one forming his or her beliefs and practices in response to the interests and pressures of others; there is an ultimate sense of comfort and security in being oneself. Yet persons at this stage are universal in their acceptance of others and ready for fellowship with individuals or groups at any of the other stages or from other religious traditions.

According to Fowler, stage 6 persons have the ability to respond to the concrete situations and individuality of persons encountered in daily life while also speaking to and evoking their potential. They seem instinctively to be able to relate to others affirmingly and supportively, ever modeling a style of life that challenges and intrigues.[8]

Persons at this stage must face a temptation to withdraw, to devote oneself to spiritual communion with the Source and Foundation of one's faith. This degree of transcendence from the concrete realities of life potentially blocks the ultimate expression of faith—that of transforming the world into an actual kingdom of God.

PERSONAL PERSPECTIVE

What impressions do you have? If you are like I am, there is a lot here that helps me understand myself; but there is still resistance to the idea of explaining faith development. Somehow I want to know, and yet I want to let it remain a mystery; I guess this is one of those cross pulls.

To gain a clearer understanding of my faith development, I began to compare my growth with the processes described by Westerhoff and Fowler. There is great similarity in the progression, as shown in figure 8.

I couldn't help but wonder, however, how growth and development could always be explained so logically, in a linear fashion from left to right. I have had so many highs and lows, advances and retreats, and spurts and plateaus in my life. Development just can't be explained in a sequential pattern. (More on this later!)

As I put these growth patterns together, the similarity they have with the natural development and potential of a human being at various points in life is uncanny. The *possibility* for faith—one's way of knowing—seems to parallel the opportunities a person has to appropriate knowledge, attitudes, and skills related to *any* part of life. This potential appears to me to be a part of creation—innate in every individual.

Thus, the religion one develops as a young child is appropriated as a natural part of the total learning experience, right along with such things as what tastes good and bad, ways to get attention, and behavior which is right or wrong.

I was reminded of Paul's reflections on his spiritual growth; when a child, he spoke and thought like a child; but as an adult he gave up childish ways. The parallel experience in faith is to see through a glass darkly when immature, and gradually to see more clearly and distinctly. (See 1 Cor. 13:11-12.)

This picture of growth illuminates Paul's statements about the direction of spiritual development being an ongoing process,

The Process of Faith Development

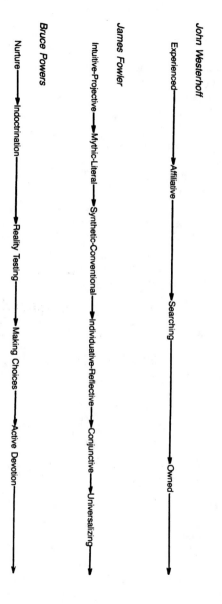

John Westerhoff

Experienced ──────► Affiliative ──────► Searching ──────► Owned ──────►

James Fowler

Intuitive-Projective ──► Mythic-Literal ──► Synthetic-Conventional ──► Individuative-Reflective ──► Conjunctive ──► Universalizing ──►

Bruce Powers

Nurture ──► Indoctrination ──── Reality Testing ──── Making Choices ──── Active Devotion ──────►

Figure 8

aimed toward fullness or maturity in Christ. (For example, see Eph. 4:13 and Phil. 2:12.)

A progressive, maturing experience in the Christian faith appears to be not only acceptable but *expected* of persons choosing to follow Christ.

Another point of interest focused on Fowler's claims that persons at one level of faith have difficulty understanding or relating to subsequent stages. There is an approach-avoidance tension, or conflict, with the next stage as one begins to see some of the issues involved; but understanding is minimal, and for further stages impossible.

This led to an examination of some passages which might illustrate various levels of faith development. Frankly, I was quite intrigued at the possibilities this holds for insight concerning the various ways in which Jesus interacted with people in his teaching as well as ways in which teachers today communicate in Bible study classes. Here is what I found.

STAGE 1—INTUITIVE-PROJECTIVE FAITH

The household baptism mentioned in Acts 16:30-33 seems to apply to this level of faith. Surely we could expect the children to come under the influence of the head of the household in faith as in all other matters.

Another example is in Matthew 18:3, where Jesus pointedly advises that the beginning of faith requires a childlike experience. To the nonbeliever, this may have appeared a joking matter: How can one become a child again? To believers, however, there was clarity in seeing that the path to growth involves an initial childlike awareness of, devotion to, and dependence on God in Christ.

This simple expression of faith is what we often see in children between the ages of four and seven, who have grown up in a Christian home. Their faith is a natural part of life, a reflection of the nurture with which they have been surrounded.

STAGE 2—MYTHIC-LITERAL FAITH

The emphasis on rules and literal interpretations in this stage perhaps is best illustrated by the giving of the Ten Commandments in the Old Testament (Ex. 20), and by the Sermon on the Mount in the New Testament (Matt. 5—7).

Wherever there is the claim of authority or the description of rules, the best hearing and response is gained from those at this stage. In each of these cases, the people in general had an intuitive faith but had not yet translated this into a set of rules by which they would be judged.

Faith at this stage can be observed first in one's life usually between ages seven and eleven. Here, the rules for everything become very important. There are no gray areas; there must always be an authoritative answer. (Have you ever seen kids spend as much time arguing over the rules as they do playing a game?) Literal interpretation of the Bible and any other *authority* source such as a book, newspaper, preacher, teacher, or policeman is an expected part of this stage.

STAGE 3—SYNTHETIC-CONVENTIONAL FAITH

This stage can best be identified when there is a *we versus they* distinction, such as illustrated in Acts 15 by the existence of a circumcision party. These persons felt that in order to be a disciple of Christ, one must first be circumcised; this was the conventional viewpoint regarding the rules of faith.

Peter also struggled with this issue, illustrating a transitional tension (being drawn toward the next stage) as described in Acts 10 and 11. He held the conventional viewpoint, but was exposed to new understandings that required him to respond. Peter chose to move from his *we versus they* (Jews vs. Gentiles) distinction to a *personal* conviction that Jesus Christ was for all persons.

The peer orientation usually becomes evident as persons reach twelve years old, and can be a dominant influence throughout life. As individuals learn the conventional way of viewing life in their cultural-faith tradition, they pattern their lives according to the norms expressed by the important persons and groups. Thus, a person can fit in and find security and acceptance. Those who meet the criteria are the we group, and those who differ are the they group. Remember the peer groups (or gangs) that became important as you reached middle-school years? And can you also recognize some of the same *we vs. they* competitiveness among adults in religious, political, or social groups?

STAGE 4—INDIVIDUATIVE-REFLECTIVE FAITH

As in Peter's faith development, there must be exposure to information or experiences which cause one to rethink conventional, group-oriented patterns in order to move into this stage. There must be a *reorientation* wherein the individual consciously separates from the group and develops *personal convictions.*

The reorientation aspect might be compared with Jesus' challenges: you have heard that it was said; or the current religious practice is . . . , but I say to you . . . (See Matt. 5-6.)

The personal conviction comes as one is able to identify what others believe or think, then make one's own commitment, such as illustrated in Simon Peter's confession, "Thou art the Christ, the Son of the living God" (Matt. 16:16, KJV).

Searching often characterizes this stage, as one examines the various alternatives for belief and practice. It is not necessary that options be radically different (although they might be), just that the individual takes seriously the inquiry and decision-making. The choice to move from a *we-believe faith to an I-believe faith* is the critical step in developing a personal relationship with God.

An example of one who was searching but could not sufficiently reorient his values is the rich young man who asked Jesus how he might have eternal life (Matt. 19:16-22). As you may recall, he declared that he had kept the religious commandments from his youth up; but he could not sell his possessions, give to the poor, and follow Jesus. Another example is in John 12:42: individuals believed on Jesus, but did not confess it lest they be rejected by others.

The move toward individualizing faith generally is associated with post-high school, moving away from home, beginning a vocation, and other such separation experiences, thus it might be observed beginning about age eighteen.

STAGE 5—CONJUNCTIVE FAITH

The paradoxes of faith often escape us, for they represent the ability to accept the illogical and to affirm the unknowable. Such is the maturity required of the religious people in Jesus' time to understand his assertion, "He who believes in me, believes not in me but in him who sent me. And he who sees me sees him who sent me" (John 12:44-45, RSV).

And how can one truly accept the full divinity *and* full humanity of Jesus, or the concept of the Trinity—God as Father *and* Son *and* Spirit—without the capacity provided by this level of faith?

Until a believer is ready for this stage, Jesus' teachings concerning *love your enemies* (Luke 6:27); *turn the other cheek* (Luke 6:29); *he who believes on me doesn't believe on me, but on him who sent me* (John 12:44); *whoever will save his life shall lose it, and whoever loses his life for my sake shall find it* (Matt. 16:25); *and whosoever will be leader must be servant* (Matt. 20:27) have little meaning. They are mysteries, accepted perhaps because of the authority of the teacher, but not incorporated into one's understanding, commitment, and practice.

Perhaps the clearest and most apt biblical illustration of conjunctive faith is found in Paul's imagery of the church as the body of Christ. There is uniqueness and strength in every part, yet none can have full expression without being combined with others. In short, there is unity and integrity *because* of the diversity; wholeness comes at the cost and risk of differences (1 Cor. 12).

STAGE 6—UNIVERSALIZING FAITH

Faith at this stage has the capacity to participate in the movement and intent of God without regard to time, place, or persons involved. In addition to having made a personal faith pilgrimage, one at this level can affirm, inspire, and have fellowship with persons at any other level without regard to social, religious, political, or economic barriers. This was part of Jesus' ministry. His life demonstrated how best to speak to the needs and concerns of all people, with utmost respect for their situations and personal integrity; this he did without undue concern for his own well-being. One of the best illustrations of this is the encounter involving Jesus, a woman caught in adultery, and her accusers (John 8:3-11).

A growing faith that reaches this level of maturity can clearly understand and build life upon the great claims of the Christian faith, such as "Jesus Christ is Lord" (Phil. 2:11), "God is love" (1 John 4:8), and "In the beginning was the Word, and the Word was with God, and the Word was God" (John 1:1).

The outcome of the faith journey can best be summarized in the words of Paul: "until we all attain to the unity of the faith and of the knowledge of the Son of God, to mature manhood, to the measure of the stature of the fulness of Christ" (Eph. 4:13, RSV).

THE UNDERLYING PROCESS

All of this makes sense as long as we don't ask too many questions. And that is just the problem, I guess, with our trying to understand faith. We can describe how it appears, yet finally we must accept our observations as finite and incomplete reflections of a vast, incomprehensible, and awe-inspiring process.

But I cannot pass this point without making an observation. Faith development cannot simply progress from level to level, from young to old, from simple to complex, from known to assumed, and from experienced to owned in a sequential process. The content and practice of my faith doesn't come in a neat box; I continually discover more and different things which must

A Learning Process

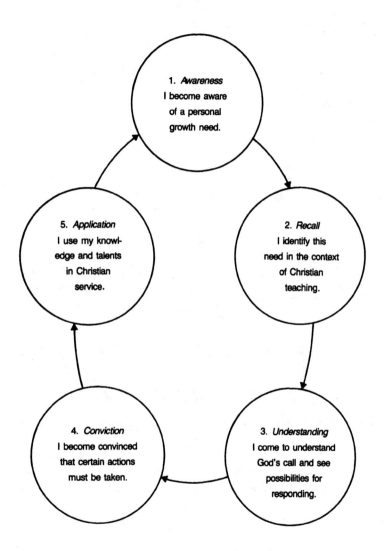

Figure 9

be considered. Consequently, I sometimes can see myself in *several stages at the same time* depending on the area of growth in my life. Also, I am sure that at each growth point as I develop new understandings and refine old ones that I *regress* as I try to nail down specific meanings and interpretations.

So, this being said, let me give you *my interpretation* which at this point helps me accept these theories of how faith grows.

Underlying a general progression in faith development is a cyclical learning process that continually enables a person to adjust to life needs. As illustrated in figure 9, the cycle is a simple five-step procedure that is the foundation for all natural learning. It is ongoing, and related to every experience in one's life.

This cyclical learning process, it seems to me, must be viewed as the foundation for sequential faith development stages. This learning process creates the *potential* for faith development, and becomes the tool by which individuals can influence the quality and degree of faith which is attained. Hence, a clearer understanding of how one's faith grows can be illustrated by a combination of faith stages and the learning process, as in figure 10.

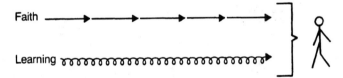

Figure 10

So important is this learning process (how teachers, leaders, and parents, influence faith development), that I have chosen to focus on this in a subsequent chapter rather than discussing it as a part of this section.

SUMMARY

Faith development is a process unique to every individual. And yet there are enough experiences which are common to all persons that we are able to identify patterns of growth. These patterns are sequential and developmental: each growth step builds on that which has gone before, but gives new character and interpretation to the whole.

Underlying this process is the ongoing mystery of 1) how and why God encounters individuals in so many different ways at so many different points in life, and 2) the role of parents, teachers, and leaders as mediators.

A model for interpreting the growth of faith as a natural part of one's religious education was suggested, integrating *faith development* as sequential stages and *learning* as a cyclical, facilitating support system.

LEARNING ACTIVITIES

1. Complete the following sentences. If you are studying this with a group, share your responses and give your reasons.
   A. My current religious experience is most like the description of _____faith.
   B. Right now, I am _____

   _____

   about where I see myself as a disciple.
   C. The issues I am facing are: _____

   _____

   _____

2. Describe your reaction to the faith development processes. How do they compare with your experience? _____

   _____

   _____

   _____

   _____

3. Drawing from your understanding of the way faith develops, interpret Acts 15:1-35. List the key ideas: _____

   _____

   _____

   _____

4. How does the learning process illustrated in figures 9 and 10

relate to Peter's experience in Acts 10-11? _____

_____

_____

_____

4
The Christian Witness

What are we trying to do to people? Consider this as a possible answer. The purpose of educational ministry is to develop within persons an understanding of, commitment to, and ability to practice Christian teachings. Another way to view this is to describe Christian education as the ongoing efforts of believers seeking to understand, practice, and propagate God's revelation.

Seminary teacher, age 41
Former minister of Christian education

What *are* you trying to do to people? A Christian's faith ultimately must be judged by standards generally claimed by those who profess to be disciples of Jesus, the Christ. These standards at best are accurate interpretations of the message proclaimed by Jesus and incarnated in the beliefs and practices of the church. However, as we have seen, faith takes on many forms, not the least of which are the norms for one's faith community. Consequently, it would be difficult to say that there is any one prescribed set of beliefs and practices that represents the *true faith* to be passed on to future generations.

What we do seek to pass on is our best interpretation of how we have experienced God, realizing that our human insight has a very limited perspective. Nevertheless, what we have is real and true for us; it is this revelation—what we know, what we feel, what we do—which becomes the predominant influence that we seek to exert on the young and on those whose beliefs and practices are different.

GROWING FAITH IN OTHERS

We influence faith development in others through two primary means: direct intervention and example. Direct intervention is an action taken by one person in an effort to influence another. For example, a parent makes a direct intervention when he or she tells a child how to behave or enrolls the child in Bible school. The initiative is with the person who seeks to give or develop in others the knowledge, attitudes, or skills considered important.

Teachers and preachers are prime examples of persons who often seek by direct means to influence the lives of others. Actions are usually direct—such as a lecture, sermon, or testimony—and often in the context of a planned encounter, such as a Bible class, worship service, or visit to someone's home.

How one responds to the direct intervention of another varies. Consider these three situations.

1. A young lady, nicely dressed, knocks at your door. She tells you she is taking a survey of the neighborhood to find persons who would like to be part of a religious group unfamiliar to you. She says, "If it's convenient, I'd like to come in and show you some materials and tell you about my beliefs." *How would you respond?*

2. Jimmy, a lively twelve-year-old, is enjoying himself at the church picnic. He and several cronies are teasing a younger boy who is obviously upset by the barbed comments. Knowing only Jimmy, you walk over and tell him that such behavior might hurt feelings and isn't appropriate. *How do you think Jimmy would react?*

3. In a Bible study class, the teacher places an outline on the chalkboard. Class members have been studying passages in Galatians and now are focusing on the historical setting. The teacher turns and calls attention to a specific chapter and verse, which each person finds and reads. *How are these people responding to direct influence?*

The response to direct interventions varies depending on one's interest, openness, need, and degree of trust/suspicion. Can you identify which of these are present in each of the above situations?

In the first two situations, suspicion and openness might be involved; in the third case trust and interest would be prominent. This illustrates a basic principle in seeking to influence others directly: *a person must be open and willing to be influenced.* Otherwise, one's existing resolve is strengthened in order to resist the direct intervention.

Influencing others by *example* is an indirect way to elicit change and growth. Although actions may be intentional, they represent more an expression of the beliefs one holds and are not necessarily directed toward others. The parable of the Pharisee and of the tax collector praying (Luke 18:9-14) is a good illustration. They both chose to pray, but one did it to impress and the other did it to confess. *Which one would impress you?*

Indirect influence by example, or by modeling, is possible because the human mind always seeks out discrepancies. That is, whenever there is a difference between what I know and what I would like to know, how I feel, and how I would like to feel, or what I can do and what I would like to do, I recognize a need. As I see ways others are meeting these needs, I become very impressionable and open myself to being influenced.

Thus, influence by example is powerful due to the high degree of motivation engendered in the recipient. And as one chooses to be open to another's influence, the potential for growth and learning through direct means increases proportionately.

Influence on others, then, must be approached in a combination of direct and indirect means. We must model and demonstrate in every action the faith we hold and incorporate at appropriate points direct teaching to assist others in dealing with the issues of faith.

This is a crucial issue for teachers, church leaders, parents, and others who have responsibility for assisting persons in their spiritual development. Consequently the following chapter will be devoted to the teaching-learning process as it relates to growing faith in others.

EVALUATING OUR INFLUENCE

How successful are we in passing on our faith? From a biblical viewpoint, there generally are two dimensions for evaluation: how individuals respond and how the church responds.

INDIVIDUAL RESPONSE

Our effectiveness in relating to individuals must focus on the mandate (1) that belief in Jesus is the only way to God, and (2) that believers will keep Christ's commandments. In John 14:6-17, this individual responsibility is described by Jesus as the essence of faith and practice. So, one way to evaluate our effectiveness in passing on faith is to look at how those under our influence are responding individually.

Two questions must be asked: Are persons expressing belief in Jesus? Are they living lives that are consistent with Jesus' teachings? The degree to which you can respond positively to *both* these questions illustrates your or my effectiveness in influencing individuals.

CHURCH RESPONSE

Individuals who have responded to the call of God in Christ must then focus on an added dimension to the Christian life: that persons who profess Jesus as Lord unite themselves in a body—the church—in order to carry out God's will. As Terry Young points out in *The Spirit Within You,* "The New Testament knows nothing of a free-lance kind of Christianity. Wherever you find the gospel being preached and souls being saved, it is always as a part of the life of the church."[1]

Individuals usually profess Christ as Savior after becoming acquainted with a local fellowship of believers, a *church.* It is in this environment that we relate to others and through which they come to know us. Generally speaking, we are "saved in the context of a church, and we become a part of the church so that we might share in its life and its work."[2]

What is the life and work of the church? It is the same as God's call to all Christians: to be his people and to continue the earthly ministry of Jesus. The church must be the means through which the eternal purpose of God is declared.

We can evaluate our work in this area by determining the extent to which those under our influence have become involved in the life and work of a local congregation.

WHAT ARE THE RESULTS?

Our influence, then, cannot be evaluated apart from tangible results—as individuals respond to God and as they involve themselves in a church. Naturally, we would all want to interpret the specific meaning given to the type and quality of tangible results. But the fact remains, as we seek to influence the faith development of others, *there is a response*. And that response must be judged by criteria such as those described above.

The question now comes back: How successful are we in passing on our faith?

REDESIGNING OUR WITNESS

How do you evaluate your influence as a Christian witness? If your response is like mine, there are some ways in which we have been effective but also there are some areas of shortcoming or areas which we had not previously considered.

The important thing is to recognize the discrepancies which exist between the faith we *want* to pass on and the faith we *are* passing on. Ideally, these are the same; if they are not, the points of difference represent the areas in which we may choose to redesign our witness.

PAUL'S EXPERIENCE

Consider the life of Paul. In his early adult years the focus of his religious experience was on the *form* of worship and belief.

There was little room for personal belief and individual commitment apart from following the rules of religion.

Following his Damascus Road experience, however, he began a reorientation that changed his life and furthered the growth of the church in a miraculous way.

In many ways, Paul can be viewed as an ideal example of a witness and a maturing Christian. He is one who responded fully to Jesus' call to discipleship.

But as Paul considered his own inner being and the lives of other followers, he did not see ideal disciples. Rather, he saw persons who were in need of growth, learning, experience, and maturity. And he was convinced that through the power of God they could press onward toward being like their Lord.

Ephesians 4:15-16 and Philippians 3:12-16 give us insight into Paul's view of a maturing, or growing, disciple. One is to speak the truth in love, grow up to be in and like Christ, and work effectively with other believers. The result, according to Paul, is growth of the body and a spirit of love.

The Philippians passage suggests that disciples are not fully developed or perfect just because they have chosen to follow Christ. Believers are to seek continual growth. Even those who are more mature are admonished to keep growing toward the high calling of God in Christ Jesus.

The most impressive idea from these passages is that Christian growth is not optional. For persons who choose to accept Jesus as Savior, there is no question but what they must also make him Lord of their lives. This requires growing toward Christlikeness.

Paul went through a dramatic reorientation in his faith and, consequently, in his witness. This change was so dramatic in fact that his former colleagues wanted to kill him (Acts 9:23-25), and the disciples didn't believe he was one of them (v. 26).

A radical redesign of faith perspective? Yes. But no different than the growth process you and I encounter. Each of us has a frame of reference. When new insight occurs that does not fit easily into this way of knowing, there is a *discrepancy.* We then become unsettled until we figure out how to resolve the differences. These discrepancies are the crossing points in life: opportunities for redesigning who and what we are in light of fresh discoveries.

THE NEXT STEP

You have already begun the process of redesigning your witness by reading this book. By reflecting on your experience you have affirmed many parts of your spiritual development. But you have also been faced with ways in which others who are equally committed Christians are growing faith in a different way or at a different pace.

By exploring the variety of ways God works among us, you can focus on the changes that might be appropriate or which you would like to study further. You also can identify the ways in which others have dealt with faith issues and take comfort in knowing that the feelings and thought patterns you have are a normal part of a growing faith.

This leads to making choices: Now that I know faith development is a journey, a continuous pilgrimage, what will I do? We can accept this information and file it in our memory, or we can intentionally seek to explore the issues as each of us interprets them.

If you want to explore some more with the prospect of redesigning your witness and possibly enlarging your faith horizons, let's move into the second half of *Growing Faith.*

Whereas the focus of the first half of this book has been on *understanding* faith development, the latter portion deals with skills, practices, and circumstances that can be used to facilitate a growing faith.

So if you want to increase your effectiveness as a teacher, leader, or parent—consider the following chapters as ways to influence others. On the other hand, if you're looking for ways to grow spiritually, focus on the material as ways to guide your own pilgrimage. In either case, the learning activities at the end of each chapter will be helpful.

LEARNING ACTIVITIES

1. Whose faith do you seek to influence directly? _____

_____

_____

2. How do you seek to do this? _____

_____

_____

3. Based on chapters 1 through 4, describe the response to your influence. _____

_____

_____

_____

4. How have *you* been influenced? By whom? What can you learn from the ways you have been influenced? _____

_____

_____

_____

5. What commitments do you have for faith development? ____

_____

_____

_____

5
Teaching and Faith Development

Interview with a teacher of young adults:

What methods do you use in teaching?

"I mostly lecture. Occasionally, we discuss."

Why did you choose this method?

"Well, it just seems to come naturally to me."

What do you use for preparation?

"I use the teacher's manual and several study books. Sometimes I borrow materials from the church."

What goals do you have for your teaching?

"I want people to learn more about what the Bible has to say to them. That's about it."

Do you feel your church is successful in its teaching?

"No, not really. It seems like a lot of people just seem to be uninterested in learning."

What is the problem?

"Well, people just won't grow much, and the church probably won't grow if we don't give people something to come for. We can improve by getting more people interested. We have good teachers and pretty good literature. If we can just go out and get people in we'll be OK."

Homemaker, age 53
Teacher of young adults

The interview reported above illustrates a very common view of teaching. From the methods, to the goal, to the needs—this pattern appears in many churches. What is behind this perspective, and what is the influence on faith development?

This time, rather than my telling you, let me illustrate. I am going to use a passage of Scripture for our reference. This is from

Matthew 26, beginning with verse 69; it is the passage telling about Peter's denial of Jesus:

> Peter was sitting outside in the courtyard when one of the High Priest's servant girls came to him and said, "You, too, were with Jesus of Galilee." But he denied it in front of them all. "I don't know what you are talking about," he answered, and went on out to the entrance of the courtyard. Another servant girl saw him and said to the men there, "He was with Jesus of Nazareth." Again Peter denied it and answered, "I swear that I don't know that man!" After a little while the men standing there came to Peter. "Of course you are one of them," they said. "After all, the way you speak gives you away!" Then Peter said, "I swear that I am telling the truth! May God punish me if I am not! I do not know that man!" Just then a rooster crowed, and Peter remembered what Jesus had told him: "Before the rooster crows, you will say three times that you do not know me." He went out and wept bitterly (Matt. 26: 69-75, TEV).

Now, let me ask you to do something. Without looking back, list the characters and describe the interaction that led to each of the three denials.

What were your responses? Did you experience any difficulty in recalling what happened in this well-known Scripture passage?

If you had difficulty responding, you are not alone or unusual. In fact, the usual reaction is that we were not ready or prepared for what you asked. Like one person told me, "We neither knew how the material was to be used, nor did we realize that we would have to recall any of it."

Now, think back to the average teaching situation in a church. *What learning is taking place?* The usual response when I ask this question is that, at best, people are gaining a general awareness and possibly an understanding of the subject matter. If we stopped in the middle of a session and gave an assignment similar to the one I gave you, how would the people respond?

This brings me to the focal question of this chapter: How *can* teachers and leaders be more effective? In helping people find answers, I often suggest that they begin by looking *within* themselves. This can be done by completing the following activity.

Take a few moments to recall the persons who have influenced your life in a positive way. Limit this to nonfamily members. Select three to five of these persons, the ones who have had the greatest, positive influence on your life; then write their names in the space provided below.

PERSONS WHO MOST INFLUENCED ME

Name three to five persons who have had the greatest, positive influence on your life.

_____   _____

_____   _____

_____

Questions to consider:

1. *How* did these people influence you? (What was the learning process?) _____
   _____
   _____

2. What types of things did they teach you? _____
   _____
   _____
   _____

3. What were the personal qualities of these people? _____
   _____
   _____
   _____

You now have identified some of the persons who have been the most significant in changing your life. In some way, they have elicited within you the desire to know, to believe, or to be or do something that was significant and which you now value very highly.

In reflecting on persons who have been influential in my life, I realize that these persons are life-changing teachers; they actually changed my life. Or, rather, they created opportunity for me to learn and grow.

And if all of us can identify such persons, shouldn't we also be able to identify the learning process, the personal qualities of these people, and the types of things they taught us?

See what you can discover by answering the questions on page 71. Think hard, for in this reflection is the foundation for a life-changing approach to teaching in the church. After writing your responses, consider the patterns of learning that have been most significant in your life; try to understand the factors that enable one person to influence the life of another. What conclusions can you draw?

I cannot know exactly how you responded, but based on the answers from several thousand persons in classes and in workshops, some definite patterns emerge.

(1) Although some teaching was formal, much of the learning process was more informal and relational rather than *directed* or *supervised*. Where necessary, these persons provided information, but their effectiveness was through enabling, helping, supporting, and, in general, nurturing others.

(2) The types of things most often learned were not so much related to knowing about something as they were to *being* or *doing* something.

(3) And, in response to personal qualities, you probably have about the same responses as others: characteristics such as accepting, trusting, caring, encouraging, loving, and inspiring.

Now let me ask you to reflect on this experience. If this is the way that life-changing teaching has occurred in our own lives, what can we learn about the way in which we seek to influence the lives of others? How does the usual pattern of teaching in the church compare with what we have discussed?

WHAT IS LEARNING?

What did you learn from the first part of this chapter? What did you learn about me? About yourself? About teaching?

Rather than tell you what good teaching is, I sought to help you identify it for yourself. For me to tell you would be the conventional approach to teaching and would assume that I have the answers and you don't. But I am more interested in your identifying feelings and developing attitudes about teaching rather than gaining information.

If you expected me to tell you the answers, I assume that you were a bit uneasy or disappointed. On the other hand, if you wanted to explore new directions, felt somewhat discouraged about teaching in the church, or were searching for ways to be more responsive to the needs of people or to the movement of God in your teaching, you probably were more involved. But why is it some people become very involved in learning while others are very passive? For one possible answer, let's consider the way in which learning takes place.

LEVELS OF LEARNING

There are stages or levels through which we progress when learning something: awareness, recall, understanding, conviction, and application (figure 11).[1] These levels are sequential; that is, we cannot begin learning at one level until we have achieved the previous level(s). Also, learning may stop at any point; there is nothing that assures we will continue to learn and progress to the next level.

Let me interpret and give examples of these levels of learning:

Awareness Level—Learning at this level indicates only that a

Figure 11

Levels of Learning

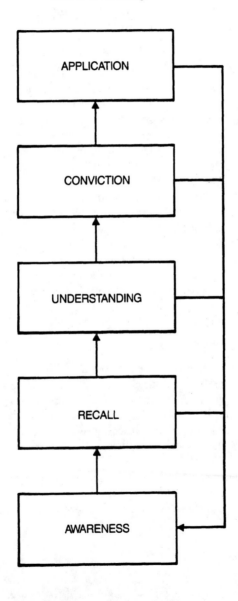

person can recognize the existence or presence of something. There is no ability to recall, interpret, or utilize the information.

For example, when reading the New Testament a person might be aware that there is a difference between apostle and disciple, but cannot give additional information.

Recall Level—Learning on this level enables a person to recall information or repeat actions in a stimulus-response manner. In other words, if asked a question, I might be able to give the answer. This level includes only recall; it does not include understanding or ability to interpret meaning.

An example of this is a two-year-old first learning to count. The child may count from one to ten but have no understanding of the meaning or purpose of counting.

Understanding Level—Once we are aware of something, and recall it when appropriate, learning can proceed to the understanding level. At this stage, we develop insights into the uses and meanings of that which we are learning. We become able to interpret and interact with what we are learning and begin to generalize the knowledge so it is useful in other situations.

An example of this is the person who, having memorized many Scripture passages, begins to see the relationships not only among the memorized passages, but to her own life—that the Bible is active in meaning and direction for her life today.

Conviction Level—Whereas the previous levels are related primarily to knowledge, or knowing about things, this level focuses on the development of attitudes and commitments regarding that which is learned. Although an attitude or feeling response may be engendered at previous levels, the learner is not really prepared to nor capable of developing informed, *personal commitments* prior to this level. After understanding, a person then, and only then, is ready and able to decide the value which will be placed on his or her learning. This is a process of clarifying and interpreting the interrelationships that the new learning has with the old.

For example, in learning how to pray, we must progress to the conviction level before we determine the extent to which it will be a part of our lives; otherwise, it is simply recall under certain circumstances. Once we have understanding, however, we can be led to determine the degree to which we *want* prayer to be a part of our lives.

Application Level—Learning at this level is dependent on a person's conviction that something is useful. Through practice and instruction, a person seeks to develop skills in using that which has been learned.

An example of this is the learning that occurs during on-the-job training.

Now I have separated these levels of learning for illustration. They are not always so distinct, but the process through which we learn is *always* the same: It begins with awareness and proceeds through the levels toward application. Let me give examples that will help clarify the progression through the learning levels:

Using John 3:16: "For God so loved the world. . . ."

- At the *awareness* level, I would learn that it exists.
- At the *recall* level, I would learn to tell it in my own words or to repeat it.
- At the *understanding* level, I would learn to describe the meaning of the verse.
- At the *conviction* level, I would determine that the message of John 3:16 is important to me.
- At the *application* level, I would act on or put the meaning of the passage into practice in my life.

In a larger context, the learning process and faith development proceed in a similar way, as illustrated in figure 12.

Figure 12
Learning and Faith Development

Awareness

God is . . .

I am . . .

A disciple . . .

The church . . .

Recall

God is Lord and Redeemer.

I am a person created by God.

A disciple is a follower of Christ.

The church is the people of God and the body of Christ.

Understanding

God saved me and is Lord of my life; therefore, I am to be a disciple, maturing in my understanding and practicing of Jesus' teachings, serving as a part of the people of God and the body of Christ.

Conviction

I want to be a disciple and am willing to pay the cost.

Application

I am involved in discovering, developing, and putting into Christian service the talents/gifts God has given me, and I am actively serving as part of the people of God and the body of Christ.

With this understanding, let me now make two observations that I would like for you to reflect upon; then I want to give some general guidelines related to learning methods. Here are the observations: First, whereas the expectations are that Christians are committed to what they study and will apply it to their lives, teaching in the church usually focuses on the first three learning levels: awareness, recall, and understanding. *It is assumed that commitment to and application of learning will take place.*

The second observation is that we often seek application of learning (for example, in witnessing, in prayer life, or in tithing) without moving through the understanding or conviction levels of learning. Consequently, teaching effectiveness is often very limited.

These observations are on page 78. Take a few moments to evaluate each statement. Do you agree or disagree? Why? Are there other observations about learning that you would like to add? Write your responses, and if studying this with a group, share your reactions with others.

OBSERVATIONS ABOUT LEARNING

1. Whereas the expectations are that Christians are committed to what they study and will apply it to their lives, teaching in the church usually focuses on the first three learning levels: awareness, recall, and understanding. We *assume* that commitment to and application of learning will take place.

2. We often seek application of learning (for example, in witnessing, in prayer life, or in tithing) without moving through the understanding or conviction levels of learning. Consequently, teaching effectiveness often is very limited.

YOUR RESPONSE

Do you agree or disagree with these observations? Why? ____
_____
_____
_____

Are there other observations about learning that you would like to add? _____
_____
_____

Did you take time to summarize your thoughts? Here are two of the insights that usually are expressed:

1. The teacher who changes lives meets people where they are and moves from there.

2. Effective teaching must encompass the total range of learning, from awareness through application. Learners cannot be expected automatically to develop commitment and make application of learning.

Now, let me share with you some information about learning methods. It is the methodology that has the greatest influence on the level and the extent of learning achieved. And this, in my judgment, is the most important function of a teacher: guiding the learning process.

Think back to the life-changing teachers you identified. Was it the subject or topic of learning that so impressed you, or, was it the *way* in which the person helped you?

I am sure it usually is a combination, but the impact of learning process is often the difference between life-changing teaching and boring teaching.

For example, as a teenager I hated to study history. I had memorized all the dates, read about all the wars, and drawn all the maps, and I was frustrated every minute. However, in graduate school I took a history course that changed my outlook about the past. We discussed events, determined how problems were handled, and sought to apply history to the solving of today's needs and the making of tomorrow's plans. History came alive for me! What happened? History as a subject had not changed; but the learning methods—and expectations of the teacher—had changed.

So, the next point I would like for you to ponder is this: The *process* through which one learns is the single greatest influence on a person's attitudes (commitments) toward the content of learning.

Do you agree or disagree with this statement? What has been your experience?

We have determined that learning includes content *and* process. These may be separate entities, but in the teaching-learning encounter, they become one as experienced by the learner. Consequently, good process can often effectively transmit weak or inadequate content, and vice versa.

But the effective teacher is a master at matching content with the appropriate method in order to achieve the level of learning desired. Look at the diagram in figure 11. Content is taught in the sequence illustrated: awareness, first; then recall, understanding, conviction, and application. Learning can proceed all the way to application, or it can stop at any point.

One key to achieving a particular level of learning is the use of appropriate methods. Some of these are listed in figure 13. For example, to achieve a knowledge outcome—awareness, recall, or understanding—the teacher would use *presentation* methods such as lecture, research and report, and question-answer.

To achieve learning at the conviction/attitude level, it is necessary to use *interaction* methods such as group discussion, role playing, and brainstorming.

To achieve learning at the application/skill level, it is necessary to provide skill-development opportunities such as workshops, demonstrations, and simulation activities.

The point is, each type of learning can be achieved most effectively by using certain methods. On the other hand, inappropriate methods are not only inefficient, they can block the very level or levels of learning desired.

Before going on, I would like for you to read the rest of the material in figure 13. Reflect on the learning methods used in your church and the ways in which you have learned as well as taught.

Figure 13
Selecting and Using Learning Methods

Type of Learning Desired	Type of Methods to Use	Examples
Knowledge	Presentation	Lecture
		Research
		Question-answer
Attitude	Interaction	Group discussion
		Role playing
		Brainstorming
Skill	Performance	Workshop
		Demonstration
		Simulation

Methods used for one type of learning can evoke learning in another category. However, in general, methods are most effective when used to secure the type of learning indicated. Each method can also be combined—and usually is combined—with other methods to provide variety and to elicit maximum response. For example, lecture and discussion are often used together.

Guidelines

1. Give clear instructions concerning what is expected. If participants are unfamiliar with a method, take time to explain. Make assignments in advance when appropriate, as in the case of research.
2. Select methods that will be most helpful in leading participants to accomplish the session aim. For example, use primarily interaction methods when seeking a change in attitude.
3. Presentation methods generally are the most *efficient* way to cover subject matter.
4. Interaction methods generally are the least efficient way to cover subject matter; however, they are the most effective

way to develop or change attitudes.

5. A combination of methods based on levels of learning desired is the best approach to group study. The worst approach is to use a method—any method—excessively.
6. When choosing methods, keep in mind
   - the ability and background of participants
   - the ability of the leader
   - the amount of time available
   - the size of the group
   - the arrangement of the meeting room
7. Secure a good reference book on learning methods to use with church groups.

HOW DO YOU DO IT?

The first step, obviously, is to develop an understanding of and commitment to being a *complete* teacher. This involves integration of the knowledge and experiences discussed thus far into *your* value system. Without some commitment on your part, this study will result only in *knowing about* life-changing teaching.

The next step is to develop an understanding of, commitment to, and skill in relating to people and in guiding group processes. For it is in this interaction with each other and with the learning content that people develop a majority of their Christian attitudes and commitments.

To give guidance, I will provide information about group leadership, then give some learning activities that either can be studied individually or used in a group. To conclude, I will suggest some guidelines for teachers and leaders.

GROUP AND LEADERSHIP ROLES[2]

Much of the Christian life is pursued in community. This is the biblical expectation—that we function as a family, or a body. Groups may be large or small, structured or unstructured, but all have as a purpose some aspect of Christian growth or ministry. The role of groups or classes therefore is to provide a means through which Christians can combine their efforts to meet common concerns related to growth and ministry.

The uniqueness of a group is that it provides a structure for sharing experiences and for developing trust and caring, all necessary for the development of values and commitments.

It is the role of leadership to assist people in (1) clarifying their purpose for being together, (2) developing guidelines for fulfilling their purpose, and (3) participating in a supportive manner.

A good leader is not a director; he or she is an enabler or facilitator of human interaction and learning. This is in direct contrast to the teacher or leader-centered style wherein control and direction are determined primarily by one person.

The basic responsibility of leadership is to bring people together. This involves not only physical presence, but common will and spirit. Generally, people have varied expectations and seem quite unsure about why they are together or how they are to proceed without being told. But through understanding leadership, expectations can be merged and cohesiveness developed in such a way that the group or class can satisfactorily achieve its purpose.

How does this happen? There are identifiable growth stages through which all groups progress. Look at the illustration in figure 14. These are the stages of group development. As a leader understands and becomes more proficient in guiding groups through these stages, meetings become more productive and people experience more pleasure in being together.

Group development moves sequentially from dependence on the leader, through counter independence, counter dependence, independence, and interdependence. Each stage is a prerequisite for the subsequent stages, and the process can always revert to the first stage. Once a group has moved through all stages, however, it may revert to an earlier stage, but it can return much more easily to the last, and most desirable, operating level: interdependency.

Here is a description of each stage. Compare this information with your observations; then I will share some of mine.

Figure 14

Stages of Group Development

(and the way group members see it)

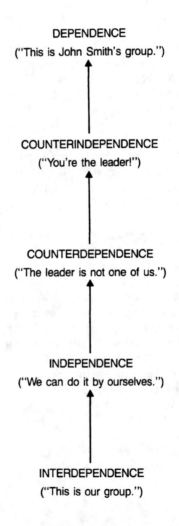

DEPENDENCE

("This is John Smith's group.")

COUNTERINDEPENDENCE

("You're the leader!")

COUNTERDEPENDENCE

("The leader is not one of us.")

INDEPENDENCE

("We can do it by ourselves.")

INTERDEPENDENCE

("This is our group.")

1. *Dependence*—"This is John Smith's group."

   This is the get-acquainted and small-talk phase of group life. Actions basically are initiated by and communication flows through the leader. Group members look to the leader to get things started.

   Comments that might be heard include: "Tell us how you want this done. Why are we together? You're the leader." When identifying the group, members often will refer to it by using the leader's name: "I'm in John Smith's group." Basically, group members feel little commitment to each other or to the group during this stage. They are dependent on John Smith, and all leadership responsibility is his.

   Many groups never develop beyond this stage, consequently individual growth and group cohesiveness are not realized. Usually, this occurs with a short-term, highly task-oriented group that meets simply to get its job done. Or, sometimes a leader, who is unaware of or unwilling to risk the potential benefits of moving to the next stage, maintains control and *directs* the group.

   People who are brought together and operate only at this stage of group development focus primarily on the task to be performed. There is little personal and group growth as might be expressed through a caring, sharing, and supportive fellowship.

2. *Counterindependence*—"You're the leader!"

   For the life-giving leader, moving the group to the second stage—counterindependence—is a prerequisite to growth for all involved. To provide opportunity for members to move to this stage, the leader begins to loose his hold on the group—providing freedom to explore, develop, and create within whatever guidelines that may exist. Members often resist these efforts due to a slight amount of tension that develops.

   A leader may suggest a sharing of expectations related to the group, or an open discussion concerning how members would like to handle meetings. Or an assignment may be given such as, "Choose two or three other people and write down five things you would like to study during the next three months." The result is often met with resistance expressed politely as, "Would you give us more information?" or, "Tell us exactly what you have in mind." In other instances, the comments may be rather pointed, such as, "You're the leader; just tell us."

This stage produces an uneasy feeling and sometimes even a hostile environment perceived both by the leader and by participants. This is normal, however, and need not frighten anyone. Leaders, unaware, sometimes stumble into this stage and become uneasy as the tension develops; they then rush to take charge and revert to the dependency stage.

An example of this is a Sunday School teacher who described to me her desire to involve her class in group discussion and other participation-type learning activities. However, she always ended up lecturing. After discussing the stages of group development, she decided that whenever she looked to the class for participation and response, she felt uncomfortable because she was not in control and members didn't always respond; this caused her always to revert to lecturing—a very controlling yet secure type of leadership.

The key to this stage is to involve members in the life and purpose of the group. Expectations are discussed, members begin to interact, and the leader gradually steps out of an *authority* role.

3. *Counterdependence*—"The leader is not one of us."

As the previous stage gives way to counterdependence, group members begin flexing their collective muscles. They begin enjoying each other and actively seek to influence the life of the group. They discover that they do not have to be dependent on the leader (or some authority figure or structure) and openly resist at opportune times. This sometimes is characterized as an adolescent rebellion: "We don't have to do it his way (or the way it has always been done)."

Members begin to think for themselves, speak openly, and direct conversation to each other rather than to the leader. Chatter is frequent, and often what the leader has to offer is lost in the interaction among members.

The danger here is that the leader will not understand this "nonproductive" behavior. To those who do not understand, this stage appears wasted time. How often I have heard a leader shout for attention or clap hands, then proceed to reestablish control over the group . . . and revert to the dependency stage, thereby squashing hopes for growth to group maturity.

During this stage, the leader simply has to endure and love—supporting but not controlling, guiding but not parenting group members. The adolescent group is reaching for maturity.

4. *Independence*—"We can do it by ourselves."

If the group is allowed to develop, a point will come when members find themselves operating apart from the influence of the leader. There will be a time or times when members speak directly to each other, make decisions, and interact oblivious to the leader. Then the group members may inform the leader what has been decided or how something will be done. The group may even choose to meet without the leader.

This stage is the most difficult for the leader to endure for the feeling is one of loss of control and even failure. The leader may perceive that his leadership is rejected or that he is not needed. Some leaders, not understanding, are hurt (and react accordingly) or venture to take control in a struggle for power. Either action produces a no-win situation.

A life-giving leader endures the group's struggle for independence and provides support, guidance, and encouragement as appropriate. He does not seek to master or regain control, for to do so would thwart the next growth step so eagerly awaited.

5. *Interdependence*—"This is our group."

As group members perceive that the leader is caring,

supportive, and not controlling, the threat diminishes and the leader becomes accepted as a member of the group *and* as leader. He is seen as a resource person and co-worker rather than as an authority figure. Leadership becomes more a function to be shared by all group members rather than invested in one person.

Cohesiveness and spirit are high in this stage, enabling the group to operate at maximum effectiveness. In addition to shared leadership, characteristics may include extensive participation and decision making by members, open discussion of ideas, sharing of concerns, increased expressions of commitment to the group, a high level of trust among participants, and an increasing willingness to venture forth into new, even high-risk, situations.

John Smith, group leader and director, has become group enabler, helper, and guide. The biggest compliment that can be paid is for members to proclaim, "Look what *we* did."

This is bringing people together. It is enabling them to become more than a collection of individuals; they become a body that in many ways has power beyond itself. In interdependence, they have the freedom to be dependent as need arises, to build on the gifts of various members, to challenge, to struggle, to share, and to achieve. An interdependent group is a life-giving group, and God in his own way can elicit a response and growth that can empower such a body to contribute their part in Christian mission and ministry.

Now let me share with you some of the thoughts I have about group development.

1. *The movement or progression through the stages may be rapid or slow.* Group development is predictable, but timing related to the various stages is imprecise due to the variety of backgrounds and interpersonal styles among members. Whereas one group may pass through all stages in a few hours, another

group will take weeks or months of interaction. And, then, some groups never progress beyond a particular stage. Leadership ability and experience of group members are the major determining factors.

Another influence on timing is the expectation each member holds related to group interaction. Persons who have experienced and value interdependence move easily toward this stage; others who have experienced primarily dependency or the tension associated with some of the intermediate stages are more resistant. The leader must be sensitive to all members, and seek to elicit understanding and development at an appropriate rate.

As necessary, this involves relating to persons individually and/or tailoring group experiences to meet a variety of expectations and needs. Since group development involves change for many people, providing opportunities for shared experience and the development of mutual trust is very important.

Effective group leaders will naturally encourage movement through the various stages. The influence of the leader will generally be greater at the beginning and gradually decrease as the group begins to mature. This progression does *not* degrade the role of the leader; it only signifies a conscious adjustment from director to enabler, from one who supervises to one who serves.

2. *The leader will experience anxiety.* Tension and anxiety can be endured if you understand it and recognize that it is a normal part of the maturing process. As groups move into the counterdependence and independence stages, a sensitive leader often feels hurt; but any move toward personally resolving the tension-producing situation will prove counterproductive. The *group* must move through the stages, with the leader guiding rather than controlling.

Knowing that anxious moments will come is helpful, but makes no less real those harsh expressions aimed at the leader. It is uncomfortable, but not unbearable. Tension is simply part of the growth process.

3. *Reflection provides an opportunity for learning.* Looking back, members can discuss feelings and share evaluations related to their growth as a group. They can explore the relationships and struggles for influence that were a part of the growth process. Such an evaluation can be done periodically in an informal way.

Even after the group has the ability to function interdependently, occasional process evaluations will strengthen and maintain the cohesiveness of the group as well as improve the study and other task-related functions. Leadership responsibility includes calling for reflection and evaluation whenever appropriate.

4. *There will always be no-grows.* Invariably you will be involved with some people who simply do not value growth—for themselves or for others. They will be the ones who always encourage dependence on the leader; they react negatively to any persons who begin to reach out in search of growth.

Fortunately, these people are usually in the minority and serve only as a minor deterrent to group development. Sometimes, however, these persons gravitate to the same group; they want a director-leader who will primarily lecture or present devotional talks. Leaders who seek learning through group participation generally experience frustration when working with such people over an extended period.

5. *Group growth parallels human growth.* The stages of group development resemble the stages through which every person moves. As infants we are totally dependent. Later, the child begins to test this dependence and to determine limits of freedom. There are urges for freedom and yet desires for boundaries during adolescent years. At some point, most people break away and test their independence. Then they desire, and feel greater freedom, to renegotiate their relationships based on interdependency—as adult to adult.

You may have other observations. In a moment I would like for you to reflect on them. Whether by yourself or in a group consider the levels at which groups and classes in your church operate. When you are leading or teaching, what happens? How do you evaluate your experiences and relations with others? *Now is a good time to pause for reflection.*

TEACHING FOR CONVICTION

The rest of this chapter will deal specifically with what I consider to be the weakest area of teaching in our churches: the development of attitudes and feelings. Thinking back to the levels of learning, this is the type of teaching that leads to *conviction.*

My observation is that churches spend the major portion of planned teaching time on the *awareness, recall,* and *understanding* levels. A distant second is the teaching time devoted to *application,* for example, through workshops, demonstrations, and on-the-job training. The major weakness, and the point of breakdown in the teaching-learning cycle, is intentional teaching that elicits learning at the *conviction* level.

This is the learning that changes lives. It is a person's feelings, attitudes, and commitments that control actions. Learning at previous levels is primarily conceptual; learning at this level is related more to emotion—the strongest influence on human behavior. If a teacher spends a majority of time seeking intellectual or skill development, chances are that few lives will be changed.

In this regard, I have one other question which I faced a few years ago: How best can *God* work through our teaching?

Does this question surprise you? I realized that as long as I directed the learning process, the class members could gain a lot of knowledge *about* things. But was that sufficient? Knowledge and skill are necessary, but God seeks *conviction* and *commitment.* I finally accepted the fact that in teaching *about* God and the Bible, I was limiting God's movement within and among his people. I realized that this dynamic interaction is the missing link in Christian education which creates the potential for life-changing results.

Thus, the role of the teacher is not to change lives; rather it is to create the opportunity for God to move in and among persons to develop the commitments and cohesiveness necessary to be, to do, and to tell the gospel.

This in no way negates the necessity of teaching for knowledge and skill development; it does, however, suggest that the teaching process must include opportunities for *all* levels of learning. And teachers must become more knowledgeable of and proficient in guiding learning at the *conviction* level.

TEACHING STRATEGY

There is no substitute for the personal qualities which a teacher or leader can bring to a group. This is the intangible aspect of giving and receiving, initiating and responding based on the felt needs of any situation—without regard to formalized techniques, formulas, or theories of leadership behavior.

However, there are those times in the life of a class or group that require more from a leader than simple guidance or support. As problems or potentially unhealthy situations arise, it is the responsibility of leadership to initiate deliberate actions designed to protect the integrity and the purpose of the group, as well as to insure the growth potential for all involved.

Such actions represent leadership strategy. They are preventive or prescriptive steps taken to avoid or to solve a problem.

Listed in figure 15 are some guidelines for teachers and group leaders.[3] Understanding and using them does not assure life-changing teaching; however, a leader's ability to avoid or to solve problems is in direct proportion to his or her ability to draw from and effectively follow such guidelines. Thus, it would be helpful to study and try out some of these actions at appropriate times. Discover those that you can use effectively and determine the circumstances most effective for each.

Figure 15
Guidelines for Teachers and Group Leaders

1. Prepare for each meeting. Determine what needs to be done and the process that will be followed.
2. Follow your plan but be open to adjustments depending on the needs of group members. Occasionally you may feel you are losing control when many people get into the discussion or when several members seem to "chase a rabbit." Resist the impulse to take charge and bring everyone back to the subject. Listen carefully and analyze the situation; members may be involved in a learning or sharing experience that is very meaningful to them. When appropriate, make a transitional statement and proceed.
3. Involve members as much as possible. People learn best when they are actively involved in the learning process.
4. When a person is dominating the discussion, bring other members in by saying, "John has shared his opinion; what are some other viewpoints?"
5. Whenever disagreement is apparent, lead members to focus on the problem or issue rather than on the people or personalities involved. For example, say, "Let's stop a minute and examine the problem; what is the issue with which we are dealing?"
6. Use the problem-solving process whenever you or the group are stuck in an uncomfortable or unsure situation:
   - Define and analyze the problem.
   - Suggest or find alternatives for solving it.
   - Evaluate the alternatives.
   - Select the alternative that seems most appropriate for solving the problem and try it.
   - If the solution is not satisfactory, repeat the process using the information gained.
7. Initially, a group will be dependent on the leader and many members will simply sit and listen to what is said. Instead of keeping the group in this dependency stage by provid-

ing all of the information and guidance, encourage group growth and participation; use discussion-encouragement techniques such as:

- What is your opinion?
- How would you do this?
- What is your reaction to this situation?
- Discuss your feelings about this with the person next to you.
- What response could our group make?

8. Watch and react nonverbally to group members as they participate. Let your face and body give indication that you are interested and that you *care*. Gradually others will unconsciously imitate this type of behavior which encourages participation and raises the level of caring among members.

9. If the session becomes disrupted, instead of acting as if nothing is wrong, simply say something like, "I am a bit uncomfortable about what is happening; how do you feel about it?" Evaluate, regroup, and then proceed.
Note: If the disruption is potentially embarrassing to someone, a different approach is needed. Seek to put the person at ease rather than leading the group to evaluate the situation. (This *may* include ignoring the disruption.) Proceed when appropriate.

10. In the case of a crucial problem that is particularly disrupting, consider using the problem-solving process. If necessary, save the planned agenda for another session.

11. Call for information, clarification, elaboration, or summary whenever appropriate. Do not assume that everyone is staying with the trend of thought and that the major points will be recognized. Involve members by saying things such as:

- Does someone have additional information?
- Bill, will you please clarify your earlier statement?

- Linda, talk a little more about that; how did you get it started?
- Lynne, would you summarize the main points that have been made?

12. Value the contribution of every person. A comment may seem to be off the subject to you, but it could be the best thought a person has had during the session and, perhaps, very important to him or even to the group. Sometimes, however, a person may become an overactive participant and restrict the participation of others. In this case, you might say tactfully, "OK, now let's hear what others have to say," or "Thank you; what do the rest of you think?"

13. Avoid "speaking for the group" unless you have been authorized to do so. Some leaders make the mistake of saying to the group things such as, "Of course, everyone in our group already is in favor of this." If this is not a fact, then this type of statement creates hostility or tension in those who disagree. A better approach would be to say, "Some may already favor this." Whenever possible, let people speak for themselves.

14. Involve members in making decisions that will affect them. This indicates that in the leader's opinion the group is important and that the contributions of each person are valued. Another benefit is that members have a stronger commitment to carry out decisions which they have helped to make.

15. Affirm and encourage the worthy contributions of members. Give praise when due and avoid blaming when things go wrong. Affirmation and praise encourage growth and participation. Blaming stiffles growth.

To conclude this chapter, I would like to share with you seven suggestions which I consider essential for effective teaching and group leadership in a church:

1. Encourage the group to discuss the purpose for being together. Establish a covenant with one another so that each person will know what to expect from the group and what will be expected in return.
2. Share responsibilities. Each member should participate in some way and contribute to the life of the group.
3. Be supportive of each other; develop a caring atmosphere.
4. Involve group members when making decisions that will affect them.
5. Evaluate periodically, keeping in mind the purpose of the group. Make changes and improvements as necessary.
6. Discuss and make plans for the time when the group may need to divide into two or more groups. Groups that really meet needs will grow. Once a group reaches an average attendance of about fifteen, consideration should be given to starting another group. Several members of the existing group could form the nucleus for a new group.
7. Help the group maintain a balanced emphasis on inreach, outreach, and upreach. Inreach—a concern for the group and for personal and spiritual growth. Outreach—a concern for reaching and ministering to others. Upreach—a concern for maintaining a dynamic relationship with God.

LEARNING ACTIVITIES

1. Complete the activities included in the chapter. If you are studying this with a group, discuss your responses with others.
2. What ideas have you gained about how we seek to influence the lives of others? How does this compare with your feelings at the end of chapter 4? _____
   _____

_____

_____

3. How does the usual pattern of teaching in the church compare with what we have studied in chapters 4 and 5? _____

_____

4. Describe a group experience that illustrates one or more of the stages of group development. How did you (or the leader) handle the situation? What would you do differently next time? _____

_____

_____

_____

5. Review the *Guidelines for Teachers and Group Leaders*, figure 15. Place a check mark by those you do now. Draw a circle by those you want to try. Discuss the merits of these suggestions and evaluate the way you have worked together if studying this with others.

6
Faith Development in Action—I

I have reflected upon my past upbringing in Christian fundamentalism as in relation to newer insights I have gained. As I look back, I find that I owe a lot to my fundamentalistic instruction in the faith. In fact, I probably would not even be where I am, as a Christian, were it not for my entrance into the faith through the door of fundamentalism. Simply put, my idea is that each Christian begins as a fundamentalist.

A former fundamentalist

Are we able to appreciate the process of Christian growth? And are we able to recognize faith as it grows in our lives and in the lives of others?

I would like now for us to focus on case studies that illustrate faith development. By reading these actual accounts of how others view their spiritual pilgrimage, we can gain new insights to guide us (1) in personal growth, and (2) in understanding, accepting, and assisting others. Then, in the closing chapter, I will suggest some positive ways to plan for faith development in one's life, family, and church.

I have selected the following material from two years of interviews, surveys, and personal journals which my students and I have compiled. Each illustrates a portion of the natural progression through the levels of spiritual development described in previous chapters. In some instances, the illustration clearly demonstrates faith at a particular level. At other times, there is a progression that can be followed.

I have arranged these in four sections that parallel the faith development process:
1. Faith—From Babes to Believers
2. Faith—A Covenant Community
3. Faith—The Community and Beyond
4. Faith—An Unlimited Perspective

At the beginning of each, I will briefly remind you of the characteristics identified with that expression of faith. At the end of each, I will use an example of someone in transition to the next phase.

As you read, look for the parallels in your life, the ways others seek to grow as Christian disciples, and the thread of faith as it moves through its various dimensions from the point of inception toward full expression in the likeness of Christ.

FAITH—FROM BABES TO BELIEVERS

This section focuses on faith from its beginning to the literal acceptance of beliefs and principles. Look for the simple, natural expressions. Cause and effect are closely related, and persons usually are highly dependent on sources of authority, such as God, parents, teachers, and rules. Caring relationships are very important. Faith usually is expressed as total dependence and reliance on God.

● FAITH AND MY FAMILY[1]

TO: Parents and Other Lovers of Preschoolers
SUBJECT: Worship

How do you explain a kite bouncing in the sky, the spinning ability of a spider, or the question-asking capacity of a preschooler? How do you begin to understand (or, perhaps, remember) the ability of a four- or five-year-old to experience God in his or her life?

Family worship in our home takes on all the colors of a preschooler's experiences. At times it is formal and includes

Bible readings, singing, and prayers. On other occasions, it is a revelation of the moment—when we realize that God is speaking to us through what we are doing or saying.

I have chosen to share some of these precious moments with you in the form of selected diary records of events over the last few months. I do this with the hope that we can rekindle our awe for the magnificent learning experiences we and our children can have as they learn to praise God.

Bruce Powers
(Thanksgiving, 1979)

Dear Diary:

God is great, and God is good;
Let us thank him for our food.
Ah—men!

Sometimes fast, sometimes slow, in a rhythm that rings of a preschooler, our family worships as four-year-old Jason prays.

How often Jean and I have wondered how best to bring our children into the Christian faith. Is it through ritual prayers, such as "God is great; God is good"? through a daily, family worship period? through Bible study at home and at church? through the nurture of loving parents? through teaching by example? or, through simply responding when questions are asked?

I am sure all of these contribute in some way to the development of a child's faith. But the question persists as each new phase of preschool life unfolds into new opportunities for spiritual and personal growth: How can I most effectively help my child develop the religious values that are so dear to me?

Dear Diary:

"Watch out for the poison ivy!" Jean cautioned Jason as they examined the trees and plants. Jason squatted for a close look, his nose not twelve inches from the three-leaved "itchy plant."

"Who planted poison ivy first, Mom?" Jean reminded him that God had made all of the trees, flowers, and plants, and that this was just part of God's world.

Jason very intently studied the plant, then looked toward the sky, and said in a firm voice, "God, kill all the poison ivy; OK, God?" Then he turned to his speechless mother, "God's going to do it!"

Dear Diary:

Bruce (our ten-year-old) finished memorizing the books of the Bible today. He was very proud, and asked at least ten times during the day, "Do you want to hear the New Testament? Do you want to hear the Old Testament?"

This reminded me of an experience two years ago when Bruce joined Royal Ambassadors. In addition to the regular meetings, the boys played in a Saturday morning basketball league. A rule was that boys had to recite the RA pledge by memory before each game in order to play.

After his first meeting and before the first game, Bruce memorized the pledge. He bounded out of his room and said, "Want to hear the RA pledge?" He recited it perfectly.

Then I said, "That's good; now tell me what it means."

He had been so proud and was so eager to please, but he could not answer—not even one word about what it meant. In the silence, we both became embarrassed. Knowing nothing better to do, I suggested that he tell me the pledge phrase by phrase, explaining as he went. The result was that he could not remember the pledge, doing it that way. He ended up crying, and I felt like I deserved an *F* on this parenting test!

How was my son developing faith? I wanted understanding, but he could provide only recall. Wait a minute! Recall or telling *about* faith experiences is the way young children express their religion. Understanding faith experiences and developing personal values require *abstract* thinking. This type of thinking does not begin to develop until adolescence. Preschoolers and elementary-age children are *concrete* in their thinking. They have to see it, touch it, hear it, and recite it.

Personal understanding and values will come later—probably during older childhood and adolescence. Younger children learn through their experiences—what they see, hear, and feel. Their faith is learned from the example of the persons with whom they come in contact.

What have I learned? I will not try to be the teacher with Bruce. I will try to let him share with me the books of the Bible as many times as he wants to, and I will encourage him to tell me how accomplishing such a worthwhile task feels.

Dear Diary:

Our family was able to worship together tonight during the vesper service. We had a visiting children's choir from Dalton, Georgia, to lead us. Jason wanted to stay in big church for the entire service. With only a little fidgeting, he made it through his first full-length church service. His doing so was a reason to celebrate! We rejoiced with him, talked about the good feelings we had as a family, and treated ourselves to ice cream.

Dear Diary:

God is great; God is good.
Thank you, God, for the trees
    and for my digger toys.
Amen.

Jason departed from his memorized prayer. Perhaps he is becoming more aware of how his family expresses thanks to God for everything, and he is trying to imitate us. *A big growth step.*

Dear Diary:

Today was Bible School. As our family gathered at the end of the day, we read the note Jason brought home:

Dear Family,

Today we talked about me and how special I am to my family! Also, about how God planned it that way. Then we heard a story about Jesus when he was a little boy, just like me.

For our artwork I got to make a crayon drawing, and then we made handprints with paint and my own two hands.

I had fun.

Love,

Jason

Mom taped Jason's handprints to the kitchen wall (the refrigerator was already covered with treasured items). Jason and Bruce told about their Bible School activities. Jean and I experienced real warm feelings about their enthusiasm and the way in which Bible School was contributing to the spiritual growth of our entire family.

Dear Diary:

I wonder what effect some disagreements among the adults in our church is having on our children. The fellowship is disrupted and adults are talking openly about it. Jean and I catch ourselves discussing the situation when the kids are around. They appear not to notice, but I can't help but worry about their picking up confused ideas about Christian love and brotherhood.

I hope healing and forgiveness will be as evident as the dissension. Children need to see (and learn) how conflict can be resolved and people can forgive and continue to care for each other. (This is a good lesson for the home as well as the church.) This is difficult to deal with; I am not sure what to say, if anything, to the children.

Dear Diary:

Promotion Sunday. Jason went to a new department that qualified him to go to big church for the children's sermon. Jean and I looked down from the choir loft and saw all those cute kids from extended session sitting on the second row. Jason beamed and gave a half-wave to his mom.

After dinner, we talked with Jason about the service. We told him how proud we were of him and the way he paid attention. I hope he sensed the value we place on congregational worship services. I do want him to *feel* and *experience* praising God without thinking that a worship service is just a time to "cut his motor off."

The treat of the day came as I tucked Jason in bed. After he sang "Twinkle, Twinkle, Little Star" for me and I sang several choruses for him, we sang together "Jesus Loves Me." Hearing his sincere, off-key affirmation—"Yes, Jesus loves me; yes, Jesus loves me!"—assures me that in his own four-year-old way he *is* making sense out of worship, and *is* developing the values that I so want to pass on.

P.S. Family worship in my life is a constant stream of formal and informal, planned and unplanned experiences in which God is praised and made known among us. Through each person's openness to these events and our sharing of their meaning in our lives, I believe God's Spirit can speak to each family member at his or her level of need and comprehension.

One thing I must confess, however. As I seek to guide my children in worship, they often become my teachers. A parent or other caring person cannot truly open oneself to the simple, direct expressions of a child's faith without being moved to examine one's adult perspective.

I thank my children for helping me to *feel* and *be* worship as well as to think and do it.

- HOUSEWIFE *(two children; age 25)*
  Where do you feel you are in your spiritual development?
  Probably about like a thirteen-year-old in normal physical development. I want to be a mature adult and I strive for that, but I seem to fluctuate.
  What are your feelings about church involvement?
  I do what I feel I ought to do as a responsible member. I'm sorry to say though that I'm afraid my involvement is in terms of obedience to God. I know God wants us at that church, and he wants us to minister where we are, but for me, my ideal church would be a local Christian community. Right now the only contact we have with the people there is on a formal level. Most of the young marrieds have apartments all over town, and there is no central place we can go for Christian fellowship. It costs too much to get a baby-sitter every time we want to go to a fellowship function. I wish there could be a local Christian community.
  Can you tell me some growth steps in your Christian life?
  First of all would be my conversion experience when I was about eighteen. I was in a bad situation, and I didn't know where to turn, so I prayed, "Lord if you are really there, please help me." Next would be the YWCA I was involved in during college. We had a strong Bible study and I knew what it was like to have sisters in Christ. Next would be my marriage, when I learned submission to authority. One summer my husband and I worked at a fundamental camp and I had to learn to submit to an older person I did not necessarily agree with. I tend to be such a rebel at times.
  Next would be my first pregnancy. I really realized that God is the Creator and that our dependency must come from him. Then next would be my miscarriage two years later. I realized then that the Lord gives and the Lord takes away, and that we have to depend on him even when we don't understand.
  Then next would be last summer when we were in extreme financial need. I learned that what he gives us is a privilege, and we have to turn over material things and needs to God, and be good stewards of what we do have.
  Next would be a conversation I had with someone yesterday. I realized I often have a critical and judgmental spirit. I need to speak the truth in love and not be so rebellious.

What do you do to grow spiritually?

First, I spend time each morning in Bible reading and prayer with my husband. After he leaves for work, I continue in prayer myself. Second in importance would be the Friday morning women's Bible study I'm involved in and Sunday morning worship services.

● RETIRED, DISABLED SCHOOL TEACHER *(female; age 50)*

I accepted the Lord when I was twelve years old. Mother was a Christian—but my sister and I accepted the Lord during a revival, and all three of us were baptized in a creek one Sunday afternoon. Then on Saturday night I read my quarterly—so on Sunday morning I would be ready to tell my teacher I had studied my lesson. When I left West Virginia, I went to Florida, and they asked me to teach a Sunday School class and that helped me grow. Then the next move brought me to North Carolina. Again they asked me to teach, and I did. That was another time of growth.

Then about nine years ago, one Saturday morning I couldn't get out of bed, and I told my husband there was no way for me to move. He got me up and to the doctor, and they said it was my heart, but I was not sick enough to stay in the hospital.

Sunday morning I taught class, but I don't remember anything about teaching. Monday I went on to school to teach. Right after the children came in I felt something happen, and I asked a little girl to go get the principal; I straightened up, and he was standing there.

I don't remember much from then on. They put me in the hospital, and they had to build me up before they could do open-heart surgery. I was in the hospital three months and in intensive care three weeks, and they battled for my life. Then when I came home, I sat in this house four months, and I said, "Lord, you're trying to tell me something."

My Sunday School class came here every Sunday, and that was a marvelous help, but while I sat here I could not read. I couldn't see the words. Then when I got to the point where I could read, even reading the Bible meant nothing to me. But as time passed, that changed. One class came and a verse in the lesson that day about how God would remove the stony heart and put in one of love said something to me. God told me there was something I was leaving out.

I tried to go back to teach at school in May, and in those weeks my sister and I were called home for my daddy's surgery; he had cancer, and they could only sew him up. From that day on I stayed and took care of him—not knowing how I could do it physically or spiritually. I never slept. After three weeks we moved him home, and then I drove him every day 120 miles to get his chemotherapy.

A few weeks later, mother fell and broke her arm. So I had both of them to care for. But the Lord gave me strength as father died, and then I stayed on with mother a while after that.

I returned to teaching, but another valve in my heart wore out and I had to go back for the second open-heart surgery. But this time I went for a purpose. There was someone at that hospital who needed me. So this time when I went, I took my "Lord's artillery" with me. I took all kinds of tracts and little books. I had prayed the Lord would give me the right things to take. One day I found a little tract called "Let Not Your Heart Be Troubled," and I spread these around in my room to give to people who came in to work on me and talk to me.

The day I was to be operated on I witnessed to a girl, and she was saved. She left while I was in recovery, and I could never find her.

Again I stayed in the hospital three months, and they battled for my life because I'm a free bleeder. A week later they had to do lung surgery because I quit breathing. So through all of this I was able to witness.

While I was home recuperating, it came to me that maybe I was just going to sit there, and the Lord would bring a few people to me in my home to witness to. I looked for ways to witness right here in this house and at my front door. I made a list of ways to witness.

Then later on I realized there were many people in our church whom I did not know. So I sat down and made a list of two hundred names of women on our church roll who did not come to church for many reasons. I began to visit and pray for these ladies. I began to (for the first time) read my Bible through in a systematic way, and that's when I began my prayer list. That was in 1979. Those two things have done much to help me grow spiritually.

Through our neighborhood Bible study I have found a lady to minister to as she teaches me piano lessons. Our pastor's teachings have also helped me. Last October I left my old Sunday School class and began a new Sunday School class for those ladies that God had been sending me to—from that list of two hundred names.

Our ministry is growing, and we are finding new strength in God every day.

FAITH—A COVENANT COMMUNITY

This section focuses on faith as it is influenced by and merged with the current and historical beliefs and practices of a local congregation. Literal interpretation and authority orientation may be redirected by values and practices of this community of faith.

Notice the shift to community or peer values—the concern for right ways of viewing God and of being Christian. Participation in congregational activities, for example, is seen as a major characteristic of spiritual life. Church often is viewed as a place or an organization to which one can give service and loyalty in fulfillment of Christian calling. Social relationships and peer pressure are major influences on the degree and quality of one's faith.

● ADULT SUNDAY SCHOOL TEACHER (*married; two grown children; female; age 54*)

What age did you accept Christ?

When I was about twelve years old.

Is church a big part of your life?

Very big. I feel like I have to put church activities before anything else. And I enjoy doing what I do. I don't feel like it's a job; I do it because I want to. The church is what makes me feel like I can accomplish what God intended for me to be. I wouldn't do it on my own; it's through the church that I can see the purpose in my life.

Can you give an example?

Yes, when we lost our crop in 1960 to a hail storm, and then the very next year the house burned. My belief in Christ helped pull me through this.

When a problem or crisis arises, what do you do?

I just have to pray. I wonder sometimes when people don't do that, how do they get through it?

How often do you feel like you communicate with God?

Not as often as I should, but every day just about. I may miss a day sometimes.

What do you have to do to communicate with God?

Well, I just pour out my heart to him and I feel better. I talk with him while I do the dishes, or while I'm drinking a cup of coffee, or late at night when I'm up by myself.

What type of situation do you have to be in before you talk to him?

Well, maybe there's been some type of problem, a sickness in the family or something in the neighborhood that disturbs me, and I just talk about it. I feel better afterward.

● RETIRED DEACON *(male; older adult)*

Where do you see yourself spiritually?

Well, my church involvement started when I was a child. My family always went to church. I was baptized when I was seventeen years old and participated regularly in the church. The Training Union program was the big thing for the high school kids when I was growing up, so I attended that and was even appointed captain of my group. Then, a little later when I was twenty-two years old, I was ordained as a deacon. I served off and on as a deacon until the last three years when I began to have health problems. I was also a Sunday School teacher for fourteen years and the Sunday School director for two years. We even reached our church's record high attendance when I was serving as director.

As I mentioned before, I began to have trouble with my health about three years ago. As you know, I had this cancer in my neck. I was spiritually strengthened through this sickness. I feel that if it hadn't been for prayers, I wouldn't be here now. The doctors can't find any sign of cancer now, and I know that this is due to the treatments they gave me and the many prayers that were said—both by me and by many, many friends. Through the whole thing I never felt worried. It was like I had a faith that kept me from doubting that I would be well again someday.

Why are you where you are now?

Well, I just didn't give up. Like I said, it didn't worry me when the doctor told me about my malignancy. I just didn't lose faith. I had a feeling all the time that everything was going to be all right.

What are the characteristics of your spiritual life?

I have regular church attendance. I have always gone to Sunday School and Training Union. Participation in my church has been a major characteristic of my spiritual life. Going to church makes life happy for me. It makes me feel satisfied.

Can you identify some of your growth steps?

Being regular and faithful in church was a big step. I just always went to church because I was brought up in the church. I've heard lots of sermons and have learned lots of things there.

● CHURCH MEMBER *(female; older middle age)*

What people, things, and experiences have most influenced your faith?

I guess my association with Mrs. _____, a lady I brought to church for many years. She was a real inspiration. And preacher _____, of course.

Were your parents Christians?

My father died before I was born. My mother is a Christian.

Was your neighborhood mostly composed of Christians?

Yes.

Did the friends you grew up with affect your church life?

All my friends and schoolmates were the same in both Sunday School and school.

Has this changed with age?

It's the same. I'm surrounded with good Christian people. I just don't go where there will be other types of people.

Is social acceptance important?

Yes—among my close friends.

Do you think that society's expectations put pressure on us to deviate from Christian values?

I think it could affect the younger minds. You really have to be a strong Christian and go with groups that will uphold you.

What are some of your life goals or dreams?

I already passed my life goals. My goals were to be a help to other people and set an example for my own children and family. Also to study the Bible more. One goal I had was to take organ lessons. I was never able to.

How do these goals affect your faith life?

I had four children. During that period, you don't give as much time to the church. After that period, I put the church and church activities before all else.

● GOVERNMENT WORKER *(male; older middle age)*

How did you become a Christian?

I grew up in a Christian home. My mother was a very compassionate person. She regularly visited the sick and elderly in the church. Dad taught Sunday School. He read his Bible and prayed daily. They both spent a lot of time with me and taught me about God. They went over my Sunday School lesson with me in the week prior to church on Sunday. Before my dad died when I was nine, we used to have family devotions. After that, we didn't very much.

We were very faithful to the Presbyterian church. My family is Presbyterian from way back. When I went to college, I was not as active in church, but I still went to worship services regularly. I never really rebelled against the church.

After my father died, the pastor became my substitute father. When I was in service during World War II, he wrote me regularly once a month.

After I got out of the service I went to work and got actively involved in church. I was elected a deacon and worked some with the youth as an advisor and taught Sunday School.

I've never really had a Nicodemus experience where I felt I was "born again." I just sort of gradually grew up spiritually. I learned from my parents that Christ was important. There was never any sudden revelation to me. Just every time I open the Bible I learn something new to add on to the accumulation.

Did you ever have a turning point in your spiritual life?

I suppose the real turning point was when I was twenty-five years old and I was teaching Sunday School. As I studied the Bible, I realized that God was very real to me and that I wanted to learn more about him and serve him better. I cherish the example that my parents set for me. Because of them, God has continued to grow more and more special to me. My parents, especially my father, were very spiritual.

What is your description of a spiritual person?

That's a hard one to answer. . . . I think someone to whom Bible study and prayer (private and corporate) is important; someone who lets others know he is a professing Christian by his words and actions; and one who believes what he is doing or saying is in the name of Christ. I suppose some people in the church are hypocritical and do things for their own strokes, but I consider a spiritual person someone who is genuine . . . someone who is committed to Christ and his church.

OK . . . (interrupted)

You know, sometimes I feel like I'm not a very good Christian. I know I'm a good Presbyterian, but I'm not sure if I'm a good Christian.

What do you mean?

I think sometimes I can do or should be doing a lot more. I spend so much time in meetings at church, and I wish I could be out doing things for people to further God's kingdom. When I get frustrated though, I tell myself that doing these menial things may help others enjoy the fruits of the Spirit.

How does God speak to you?

I don't know that there is any set pattern. When I'm praying or before I read the Bible, I say "Lord, help me to hear what you have on your mind for me." Then I daydream awhile until something inside me says this will or will not work. Sometimes when there is a decision that needs to be made, I feel like it is best to just hold off for awhile and think about it. You don't have to come up with a solution right away. However, you need to get people going in what seems to be the right direction. Then if it's not right, I believe you will have a sense of uneasiness about it. You should just relax because the right thing to do will just come, at least it will be a decision that you and others can live with.

What do you do to grow spiritually?

I read the Bible every day and pray daily at different times throughout the day. I don't really have a systematic way of reading the Bible, but it's not at random either. My wife is involved in a weekly

Bible study fellowship, and I keep up with what they are studying in it. And then of course church every Sunday. We go to early service together at my church; then I go to Sunday School and she goes to her church for Bible study; then we go to the 11:00 service at her church. (His wife goes to an Episcopal church two blocks away. Note the searching and paradoxical issues; they signal a transition to another phase.)

FAITH—THE COMMUNITY AND BEYOND

This section focuses on faith as it is tested and refined by personal experience beyond the traditional boundaries of one's own peer group. Whereas authority and community were previously the strongest influences on faith, an individual's *personal* understanding of and commitment to religious concepts becomes primary. With purpose and meaning the crucial concerns, individuals seek to determine what and why they believe, and then to reorient their lives accordingly.

Notice the way in which these people ask questions, reflect on their beliefs, and seek to incorporate Christian values in their lives. Their concern is not self-centered, however; they value Christian growth for all disciples and actively encourage their congregations to be faithful to purpose and mission.

● COUNTY WORKER *(male; older adult)*
Tell me about your church involvements.

I feel I'm in a rather unique situation because I started coming to First Church soon after I was born. I've been a Sunday School teacher for twenty-seven years and have taught high-school age, ladies, and men. I am presently teaching a newly formed couples' class. I've enjoyed teaching Sunday School because I've found that though the same stories appear over and over again, I realized how complex they really are and that something new can be learned each time. It's a tremendous responsibility because people take what you say as the Bible. That's why I frequently say, "This is my interpretation . . . my own opinion." I've served on several pulpit committees. I think pulpit committees are barbaric. There's got to be a better way because pastors are bound to get hurt in this process. I'm a deacon and have served two or three terms as chairman.

What have been some of your spiritual growth steps?

My parents were a tremendous influence. Also I had an aunt who was turned down for foreign mission service but became superintendent of the Junior department. She influenced the lives of many of us kids. My years at college changed me from a stuttering, stammering country boy to one with maturity and an ability to express himself.

In terms of my spirituality . . . (pause) . . . I don't know how to say it. It's made up of lots of realizations. Christianity is not majoring on the do's and don'ts. It is a life lived in relationship to God. Life's problems aren't just yes and no situations . . . we must judge by a principle. When you put man together, you find the beginning point for solving the world's problems. Religion is one man's relationship to God. (pause) A lot needs changing in the church and in our own spiritual lives. We've got to get the man right.

To be honest with you, there were many times I went to church simply because I felt it was the thing to do. Now I believe that when you go thinking like that, sooner or later you're going to catch something.

What did you catch? What led to church being important to you?

I realized that the Christian religion is what it is because of the resurrection. I realized I was a lot like the little boy who fell out of bed and, when his mother came to check on him, said that he'd stayed too close to where he got in bed. The growth process is important. Faith and works is a matter of chronology. The Christian life should be joy. Too often we make religion a long-faced religion. We get so involved in routine activities that we just don't enjoy being Christian. I'm in favor of singing songs like the doxology and "Joy to the World" every Sunday.

● TEACHER *(female; rural background; age 38)*

What stage are you in in life?

I consider myself a young adult on the verge of middle adulthood. Perhaps I am already encountering the crisis of mid-life. At least, I am asking myself some very serious questions concerning vocational choice and the meaning of my life.

What is your current church involvement?

Because of a heavy work load and of the fact that I am currently taking courses relative to my career change, I am only involved in church at the point of Sunday worship and special services.

How do you view your faith?

I see faith personally as that which gives meaning and purpose to my life. I feel that there are paradoxes within faith. I guess I see myself at times questioning what seem to be contradictions in truth. Perhaps it is somewhat of a vulnerable time for me in that I am open to truth in positions other than my own. On the other hand, perhaps it is a time of growth for me in my faith.

What are some characteristics of your spiritual life?

As I gain understanding of myself in relation to myself, to God, and to others, I see myself becoming less self-centered and more concerned about other persons. I wish I could say that I am not selfish but I know in reality I am—the paradox is present here too. Giving to others is another characteristic. Sensitivity to persons' needs and an increasing ability to hear what people are saying also are part of this. A daily quiet time or period of meditation helps me to live my faith in the world.

What are some growth stages you can identify?

At age nine, I became a Christian and joined the church. I was influenced largely by my parents and by my pastor so my faith was basically the faith of my parents and pastor. At age fourteen, during the teenage years, I began assuming more responsibility for my personal commitments and beliefs. At age twenty-four—college years—basically I held the beliefs of my church community (I remember being defensive about my faith.) At age thirty I gained an increased awareness of the value of truth in positions other than my own. This is where I find myself now.

● SUNDAY SCHOOL TEACHER *(female; older adult)*
What has been your church leadership involvement?

I began many years ago as the Sunday School teacher for eleven-year-old girls. I have been the Church Training director, the WMU director, and the missions work group leader. I have been the Sunday School teacher for the college and career class. And now I am both the Sunday School teacher for thirty- to forty-year-old women and the church clerk.

What got you interested in volunteer church work?

I guess I was born into it. I didn't know anything else but going to both Sunday morning and Sunday evening church services when I was little. Daddy and Mom took me along with them. They didn't just drop me off and pick me up. They went to all of the Sunday School and Church Training classes and also all of the worship services. I never missed a Sunday School class session until I got sick in the seventh grade. Going to and participating in church has always been a very vital part of my life.

What is happening in your spiritual development?

I think I have more questions now than in any other period of my life. I am thinking, *Is it really worthwhile?* Is the way in which I do my living, the actions and values, worthwhile? Are they really the measuring rod, and I just don't understand? For example, I know a pastor who will be conducting a funeral. He will say things about the deceased person in a positive way, things that really don't match his life. But it is the common practice to say them. Should he really say them?

Also, are my priorities in Christian living in order? Am I really living the Christian life the way Christ would have me live? One of the reasons I am a Baptist is because of the priesthood of believers concept. But there is this feeling also in Baptist tradition that God only speaks to the pastor. But counter to this tradition, I believe that if the lines of communication are open, God and I can talk to each other without the pastor's interpretation.

What has helped you grow spiritually?

First of all my Christian family—both my parents' family and my husband-children family. Daily devotions have been very important. The devotions have not only played a very important role in my life but in my families' lives as well. My parents always had a daily devotional period. And my husband, children, and I also have devotional periods. Christian friends and their support have also been very, very important.

I have worked outside the home for many years. And my contact with people has been a great challenge. Since others at work know me as a Christian, they have come to me seeking help from the Christian perspective. This has helped me to grow spiritually, I feel.

Are there some growth steps you can identify from earlier stages of life?

The critical illness of my husband is the most life-changing incident that has moved me in growth stages. I think of that time as the most important point in my growing. I have learned to lean on God's strength to get through trying times. I remember the second day of his illness. I was looking out of his hospital room, looking at the ice on the trees and watching the sunrise. I thanked God that my husband was still alive and at that point I felt the strength of God covering me.

Then during his second surgery, there are no words that can express the amount of help my friends gave to us in encouragement, calling us, sending cards, visiting, and seeing how they could make that time be made easier for us. It was then that I realized that we as humans are God's arms extended to those who are in need. This has made my family and me adjust our lives to fit this idea. There was a lot of adjustment to do this, but it has helped us, too. Our son when he was small couldn't understand why his father couldn't play with him anymore. I heard them, both father and son, crying. My son had asked why it had to be him who was ill. I heard his father answer, "Why not?" To be able to accept things and live in spite of them is the answer. That has helped me grow. That was ten years ago. I really think that in times of need, when we are knocked to our knees, we can grow much taller spiritually.

What do you think young adult Christians need for their faith development?

Involvement. I think that so many of our young adults are pulled by worldly things. They are so much more prosperous today. They are wrapped up in material goods and pleasure, of going to the beach and mountains each weekend. They always find something more important than going to church. But with the lack of involvement in church it is hard to grow. It is hard to grow as a Christian when you're not in a Christian atmosphere. Involvement is the key. This is what helped me. I was and am still very involved in church and the local community.

- DEACON *(male; late twenties)*
  How can you know when you are maturing spiritually?

  What a good question! Uh (pause), definitely "gut level." I think you're maturing spiritually, from the day that spiritual matters matter, from the day that you start actively pursuing them. You may be very immature, but you have begun the maturation process which is open ended.

  From my point of view, I don't know of anybody who has made it. Our church (Catholic) has a great tradition of saints. None of them made it. They weren't finished. They went to their reward with unfinished business, and it is up to us to carry on. They set a great example, but the work continues ever following in the tradition of a Francis or a Benedict. They had great insights, but the world has continued to change.

  And the spiritual challenge for me is to re-incarnate—now, wait, not to reincarnate; that's got a different meaning—but to *incarnate* Christ in the world today.

  The saints did it in their day. If Francis were alive today, he'd still be seeking spiritual growth. A lot of changes have occurred since the twelfth century, but Francis was seeking spiritual maturity. He changed; he went through the Christian mystery of dying and rising and dying and rising day in and day out. He never stopped. He never said—"Enough." He continued to mature. That's the challenge that's before me, and I'm open to it. I'm still pursuing it.

- FOURTH GRADE TEACHER *(female; middle age)*
  What stage are you in in life?

  I'm in my middle years—the mid-life crisis. This period has some tension for me due to the decisions I made at an earlier stage of life. I guess I find myself questioning life choices relative to what I've done in life. I find myself wondering whether I want to spend the next twenty years teaching fourth graders, or whether I want to go back to school to acquire additional education to obtain an administrative position. I love children, but I also have good administrative skills. I guess I am continually aware of the short amount of time I have left, and I want the rest of my life to count also.

So it is a time of some confusion?
Questioning is a good way to describe it.
What is happening in your spiritual development?
I am in somewhat of a questioning period personally; probably I am more open to examine the many sides of truth at the same time. The loss of a family member a year ago has also caused me to really question my faith and to realize that it contains many paradoxes. It seems when I feel that I have some questions answered, then other questions or issues arise. Because of a certain amount of tension I have felt in the last year, it is probably one of the biggest growth periods in my life.
What are the characteristics of your spiritual life?
I do not see these in terms of church attendance or not so much in terms of the institutional church, but rather as personal characteristics. I really work at trying to be involved in the mission of Jesus in my day-to-day world, which is largely spent in the classroom. Whereas I am involved with children, this also means I am involved in families. One of the keys for me is how I relate with persons in daily life. This includes attitude, having time to listen to persons, being able to share a person's hurts, and so forth. These are basic things I try to do daily. It is so much more than just Bible reading and church attendance alone, though that is important. It really involves commitment and one's daily walk. I have a deep feeling for hurting places and persons in society, and I only hope I am learning more what it means to be a disciple.

FAITH—AN UNLIMITED PERSPECTIVE

This section focuses on faith that is rooted in a consistent set of *personal* beliefs and practices. Purpose and meaning are clear, and one's role as a Christian has been determined.

Notice the resolve in these persons, and the concern for others that transcends social, economic, and religious barriers. Faith of this type is tested, refined, and chosen with full understanding of its meaning and consequences. There is no option; one must incarnate the gospel as he or she understands it.

- RETIRED MINISTER *(male; late sixties)*
What is the focus of your life?
I have a central belief that a person needs to be changed in order to change the world. You see . . . I just have never been able to accept the *status quo*. I realize I am at home in this world, but I am not at home as well. Things are not the way they should be.
How did you come to see things in such a manner?
Oh, my father was a big influence in my life. He was constantly giving me books to read. I remember him becoming actively involved in many areas of social concern when I was growing up. The church also influenced me.
Did you ever go through a stage of rebellion against your father or the church?
No, not really. In most cases I've been able to find a congregation that allowed me the freedom to be who I felt I should be.
I take it that you value freedom very highly.
Oh, I sure do. (At this time, the interviewee described in detail his concern for and involvement in issues related to justice and freedom.)
What things do you value in faith development at this point in life?
I think reading is valuable. A person must stay informed if he is going to have some sense of justice and freedom. A person must also recognize the value of diversity. By surrounding oneself with various and diverse faiths, religions, issues, and people, one is better able to understand truth and know it when he sees it.

- HOUSEWIFE *(assists husband in his hardware store; older middle age)*
Tell me some of your past and present church activities.
I used to teach children in Sunday School, but now I coteach the couples' class. I'm in a WMU circle, but I haven't been very faithful in attending since the time they told me they didn't want to be involved in service to others—that we weren't a mission action group. Another lady and I started a prison ministry and went each Sunday. Now I'm involved in ministry to senior adults. My life has been seeing the need and acting.
What has brought you to where you are spiritually?

I grew up in a Christian home. Three illnesses brought me close to the Lord. I broke my pelvis and was bedridden for three months. Realizing I would either grow bitter or grow closer to the Lord, I rededicated my life to him as a result of this first ordeal. In 1946, I contracted encephalitis. Many with this die or, if they recover, have mental problems or are paralyzed. Through the Lord's will, I recovered. In 1958, I had an illness which was a turning point in my life—a malignancy. I promised the Lord that if I lived through this that I would follow his will wherever it led. I survived and, one Sunday morning when our pastor requested four volunteers to help start a mission, I stood up, for I felt this was something the Lord would have me do. My husband stood up, too.

Working in a mission is most rewarding. It is *truly* blood, sweat, and tears. We began our mission by meeting in a filling station. For two years we were without a pastor, but we had some fine people come in to assist. The people saw me as their pastor because I would visit in their homes and keep up constant contact. We finally presented a proposal to the sponsoring church that a full-time pastor be obtained. The request was granted and the pastor would stay at our home on the weekends. It was just glorious to be used in that way by the Lord.

I even coached the baseball team for eight years. No one else would, and it seemed important to me. Many were converted through the ball team. After we had been working in that area a while, a lady I was visiting told me one day: "Since you all have been out here, the community has changed." We even began Bible schools in the homes.

There came a point when things were pretty well established in the mission that I felt it was time for me to go back to First Church. I brought some of the children from the mission area with me occasionally. They were dark and in the 1960s this caused some to raise their eyebrows. Anyway, I can take criticism.

About this time I began the prison ministry. I still get letters from some of the inmates. I always wrote back as soon as I would get a letter. If I see a need, that's where I want to be. I want to do it not for my glory but for others.

You give so much of yourself, what keeps you going?

I have always had my husband's support. When I worked with the mission, he and I would take the children on trips—places I'm sure

they never would have gone otherwise. I also need to tell you that we
have four or five foster children, and they have made our lives richer.
I'd rather spend my money this way than by living in some swanky
house. I also like working in the yard. I pray as I work in my garden.
When I get up, I try to live very close to the Lord. Without him, you
can do nothing.
(Note: This person has a weekly ministry in two local nursing homes, a
monthly ministry at a retirement home, and an ongoing ministry to
homebound adults.)

LEARNING ACTIVITIES

1. With which case study can you most closely identify? _____
   _____
   In what ways? _____
   _____

2. In which category is this case study? _____
   Describe the characteristics of faith in this category. _____
   _____
   _____
   _____

3. Which of the above characteristics have you experienced? ___
   _____

4. Reread the case study at the *end* of the above category. This
   illustrates a person in transition to the next phase. What are
   the characteristics of transition? (What does the person begin
   doing, thinking, or feeling?) _____
   _____
   _____

5. Have you experienced any of these characteristics? In what
   ways? What might you expect in the future as your faith

continues to grow? _____

_____

_____

_____

_____

_____

_____

7
Faith Development in Action—II

The case studies related in the previous chapter illustrate faith development in four general categories. Each of the persons is on a similar journey, expressing faith appropriate for his or her circumstances. The focus in these studies, however, is on the type of faith *currently* being experienced.

I believe it would be helpful now to do two things. First, I want you to read a case study following the same person as he experiences *each* of the categories. Then, I want to share with you information from the larger study which will interpret and place in context much of that which has been observed in the case studies.

A GROWING FAITH

● MECHANICAL ENGINEER *(male; younger middle age)*
How long have you been a Christian?
For a little over twelve years now. I was saved during the beginning part of the school year in my senior year of high school.
What were the circumstances leading to your conversion?
Well, that is a little hard to say since my salvation experience has a lot of strange twists to it.
Go ahead and relate these circumstances to me.
It was late October, and our church was having its fall revival. My family had been attending that church since January of that year, and my family was a real concern of the pastor of the church. That church was fundamental in its beliefs and placed a great emphasis upon evangelism. So the pastor was concerned about the salvation of my

family despite the fact that this was a church of about two thousand members. Anyway, at the end of his services, the pastor always asked for persons to raise their hands if they were saved. My family and I could not raise our hands to this question.

One night, right after the revival service had ended, we had just gotten home, and all of a sudden the pastor came to the door. I guess he stayed until two or three in the morning and led my parents to Christ.

Then I decided that I wanted to be a Christian, too, since my parents had been converted. The following Sunday, I went up front to confess and receive Christ as my Savior. Here is where this thing gets sticky. I had a crush on a good-looking girl in our youth group who was a steadfast Christian and would not date non-Christians. Thus, I got saved and baptized so that I would be able to date this girl. (I had an ulterior motive in being converted.)

When things fell apart between that girl and me, I didn't want any part of the Lord either. A few months later, I read in the paper where a pro football player blamed his struggles on being out of fellowship with the Lord, and now that he was back in fellowship with the Lord, he was a star and was going to the Super Bowl. Well, this got me thinking, and I decided that things weren't quite right in my life, so I rededicated my life to the Lord. From that moment on, I knew for sure that I was a Christian.

Would you describe your conversion as sudden or gradual?

I would describe it as a gradual process for me. When I first received Christ, I didn't really know what I was doing. During the following months, I began to realize what being a Christian was and was able to gradually make a better and closer commitment to the Lord.

Who were the key people in your conversion experience?

The pastor of the church, the youth minister, my parents, and that football player.

Why these persons?

The pastor, because of his evangelistic concern for my family and others. The youth minister, because of the model he was to me, and because he got me involved in the activities of the church. My parents, because I really did not acknowledge my need of salvation until they got saved. Finally, the football player whom I read about, because he led me to make a real and lasting commitment to the Lord.

What feelings did you have when you were converted?

To tell the truth, I was kind of nervous. I didn't know exactly what I was getting into, and I didn't know how others would react to me. I also felt relieved—from knowing that I would not go to hell now (my church stressed this fact) and in knowing that my sins were forgiven. I experienced comfort, joy, warmth, and nervousness.

Have you ever backslidden?

Oh, yes.

Describe your backsliding, if you don't mind.

I guess I have backslidden a little on a number of occasions, but the worst time I remember is during my college days. I maintained Christian friends while at college and was involved in the Navigators and other Christian activities, but I was not right in my relationship with the Lord. I was very sporadic in having my quiet time with the Lord and often neglected him completely. I kind of put my studies and my social life ahead of the Lord. In this time of backsliding, it wasn't that I was doing things that were wrong or that I was sinning grossly; it was just that I was not experiencing any Christian growth and was neglecting my relationship with the Lord.

Have you experienced any doubt in your Christian life?

Definitely. There have been times when I wondered if God does actually exist. He seemed so far away and so unbelievable, especially when I was in college. After taking one class, I thought that religion might just be a psychological phenomena in which a person deludes himself in believing in God. Whenever I experience a crisis, I wonder where God is in all of this, as he seems so distant. But I think that such experiences have served to strengthen my faith.

In what ways do these experiences strengthen your faith?

Well, after coming through these periods and maintaining my faith, I see how foolish my thoughts at that time were, and I gain a new confidence in the reality of the Lord and his concern for me. In such times, I look back to remember the periods when the Lord was active in my life and when he made miracles occur in my life.

What practices helped you grow spiritually?

I think regular church attendance and being involved with other

Christians is the main thing. The work I do in the church reminds me of the fact that I must seek to grow spiritually every day. A daily quiet time with the Lord has also helped me immensely—a time in which I pray and meditate upon devotional Scripture readings.

What Christian activities are you involved in?

I teach the adult Sunday School class in our church. I lead Church Training for our teenagers. I am an usher. I am involved with the youth of the church in both social activities and Bible study. I also assist in leading the morning worship service.

Do you share your faith with non-Christians?

Yes, I do.

How often do you do this?

Whenever possible. I usually do this at work during lunchtime. I think it is important for a person to witness to others.

Currently, what does Christ mean to you?

He is everything to me. I view him as my Lord and Savior, who rescued me from my perilous situation. He has changed my entire way of living, and is my main purpose for living. I love him dearly because he loves me so.

What hope does your Christian faith offer you?

It gives me a goal to live for—the life hereafter. When things go badly for me in this life, I know that God is there to comfort and look after me and that these sufferings are just minor setbacks.

How does your Christian faith help you deal with life?

It helps me immensely. When I suffer setbacks in the secular world, such as problems at work, in my family relationships, or in the ordinary hustle and bustle of everyday life, my faith gives me something to lean back on. If I didn't have my faith, problems in the world would get me very depressed and probably give me ulcers. However, because of my faith, I am able to find comfort and peace in even the most trying of circumstances.

What problems have you experienced in your Christian pilgrimage?

The biggest problem is knowing what the Lord would have me to do in my life. There are times that I wonder if I should be in the ministry full-time. Knowing the exact will of God is important to me, but it is so hard to know if you are doing it sometimes. All I can do is follow what I know to be God's will for me and follow the leading of the Holy Spirit and the teachings of the Scriptures.

Do you consider yourself to be growing in the faith?

Very much so. Each day provides an opportunity to grow, and when I read the Scriptures, I learn new things about God, how I should live my life, and various other things. This growth is slow, but when I look back over a number of months or years, I can see definite growth.

How would you compare your spiritual life today to your spiritual life five years ago?

I see a great change. I used to think that being moral and being Christian were the same. The church always preached against smoking, drinking, dancing, and so forth. I felt that I was a great Christian by the mere fact that I did not do any of these sins. If I saw some other person do any of these things, I said to myself, "Boy, is he some kind of horrible sinner." Now, I think that ethics should be a *result* of a person's relationship with God rather than be the *basis* of that relationship.

I used to be intolerant with persons of other denominations and religious beliefs, but that has now changed. The only thing I see as important now is that a person has a relationship with God through Jesus Christ. I now see Christianity as a matter of relationship rather than a matter of morals.

As a result of this I think I am now better able to serve the Lord, and now have more love for God and others. God is a God of love. I now have a better knowledge and understanding of the Scriptures.

Do you see God actively at work in your life today?

Yes, I do. I can see where he has and is leading me along the path which he has mapped out for me in my life. This is very comforting and reassuring to me. I have a God who loves me and has some good things in store for me. I also seek to allow God to work through me in helping others and leading them to Christ.

What is the best part about being a Christian?

It is the feeling of being accepted and loved by God even though I have been a sinner and have really let God down at times.

Do you ever feel that your being a Christian has caused you to miss some things in life?

I used to think that. I used to think, *Boy, if only I wasn't a Christian, I could be out really enjoying life and having a good time like everyone else.* I don't have such thoughts or regrets anymore. I now see that what God demands and wants from us is for our own

good. They are because God loves us and wants the best for us.
What do you see as being the responsibilities of a Christian?
I think our main responsibility is to follow the command in
Matthew 22:37-39, to love God with all our hearts and to love others
as ourselves. We should care for others and their needs. I think we
need to let others know of God's love for them.

HOW CHRISTIANS VIEW THEIR FAITH

The ongoing study project, from which the above cases were
taken, includes interviews and surveys which to date have
involved over six hundred people in more than fifty churches.
The *interviews* focus specifically on persons affirmed by peers as
expressing a high level of spiritual maturity and Christian
devotion.

The *surveys* on the other hand are conducted indiscriminately
among church-related adults and older adolescents. The intent is
to expose these persons to the various levels of faith listed in
figure 16, and then to determine how each one perceived his or
her level of development.

Through such a descriptive study, I am seeking to compile a
sufficiently large and representative sample in order to suggest
how evangelical Christians view their spiritual development.

It is risky to draw conclusions from such a highly subjective
study, but there are some emerging patterns which I believe
provide insight for church leaders, teachers, and parents. It is this
information which I would like for you to consider, but not as *the*
answer to how Christians view their faith. Rather it is a tentative
projection that will help us ask better questions as we seek the best
ways to facilitate a growing faith among those under our influence.

EMERGING PATTERNS

Take a few moments to acquaint yourself with the information in
figure 16. Notice the percentage of persons surveyed who are in

Figure 16
Categories of Faith

	1. Babes to Believers	2. Covenant Community		3. Community and Beyond		4. Unlimited Perspective	Undecided
Fowler	Intuitive	Literal	Conventional (Peer)	Individuative	Conjunctive (Paradoxical)	Universalizing	
Westerhoff	Experienced	Affiliative		Searching		Owned	
Powers	Nurture	Indoctrination		Reality Testing	Making Choices	Active Devotion	
Task to be Achieved	Respond	Affiliate		Individualize		Generalize	
% of Persons Surveyed	24.8%	24.7%		14.1%		25.1%	11.3%
Average Age of Respondents	39.99	40.92		36.59		35.59	49.78
Average Age at Baptism	13.72	13.88		13.52		12.88	16.9

each category, the average age for each category, and the average age of baptism for each group. Also look at the data for persons who were undecided, that is they chose more than one category or did not choose any.

Drawing from this study, let me share with you some observations related to our leadership responsibilities. I realize the risk in generalizing, nevertheless I propose these as tentative conclusions that merit consideration and further study.

1. About one half of the older adolescents and adults in our churches are in a fairly traditional faith orientation (categories 1 and 2) that focuses on intuition, participation, recall, and dependency.

2. About one out of every seven persons (14.1 percent) will view him or herself as a searcher, or seeker (category 3). Such a person will acknowledge doubts to trusted persons and will look for purpose and meaning in the beliefs and practices of the institution. Their faith focuses on individual integrity, acceptance of paradoxes, understanding of cause/effect relationships, and faithfulness to religion as a spiritual pilgrimage.

3. About one fourth (25.1 percent) have identified with an active, experiential faith that could be identified as experienced, tested, examined, chosen, and owned (category 4). This would focus on personal conviction, appreciation of the way one's faith influences all of life, acceptance of brothers and sisters in Christ regardless of their denominational, cultural, or economic position, and active involvement in using faith principles in all of life.

4. Attention needs to be given to the design of educational experiences in a church in order to speak to these three distinct groups. It seems that most provisions (resources, training of leaders/teachers, expectations, etc.) are geared toward the 49.5 percent in the first two categories.

5. Searching is a very critical phase (category 3). It is often threatening to others. The smaller number (14.1 percent) who actually identified themselves at this level tends to suggest a

lack of understanding and/or acceptance of this stage as a legitimate expression of true faith. Do we need to give more attention to providing for and encouraging this phase?

6. The owned faith category includes about one fourth (25.1 percent) of the persons in our churches. This group would not necessarily be more active in traditional forms of church loyalty; rather they would more likely be those who would operate out of desire and interest, giving a great deal of themselves to church and life issues deemed by them to be important. Their faith would be oriented toward effective current expression, high involvement when they are affected, action oriented rather than passive, and visionary regarding the role of the church in the community and world.

7. The age when a person was baptized does not seem to influence the level of faith one perceives he or she has attained.

8. The average age of persons in category 3 (36.59) and category 4 (35.59) is less than the average for the other stages. In reviewing the data, many young adults selected these levels. Although research suggests that persons actually functioning at these levels are middle age and older, the idealism of younger persons often causes them to identify with these levels. The point is, this is how they view themselves and their faith; it is real for them.

9. The undecided group (11.3 percent) presents a special challenge. It appears they lack specific focus on interpreting their faith, and they vary significantly from others in age and in average age at the time of baptism. In follow-up interviews with some of these persons, there was a general lack of clarity regarding one's faith concepts and/or a reluctance to discuss anything specific about personal religious beliefs and experiences.

My guess is that these persons have had limited exposure to effective religious instruction (indoctrination). Their knowledge of and experience in the faith has been assumed by them and by others to be similar to other believers. Perhaps their religious concepts developed through trial and error in the social context of congregational life.

A CONGREGATIONAL PERSPECTIVE

Although the patterns described above are the result of individual responses from many different churches, there is another way to look at how Christians view their faith. A leader, using the criteria presented earlier, can determine the profile for a group or congregation based on his or her knowledge of each person.

This was suggested to me by a pastor who has been serving a rural, small-town church for seven years. Using James Fowler's six stages, he evaluated the level of development for each of the church's 136 resident members. As shown in figure 17, he found that 59 percent express their faith either in an intuitive or a literal

Figure 17

Stages of Faith in a Rural Congregation of 136 Members

Stage	1	2	3	4	5	6
Ages 12-20	20	11	7	4	—	—
Ages 21-45	10	21	7	8	5	—
Ages 46 up	—	18	6	14	3	2
Totals	30	50	20	26	8	2
	(22%)	(37%)	(15%)	(19%)	(6%)	(1%)

way (stages 1 and 2), and that only 15 percent express a conventional orientation (stage 3). The searchers and others functioning more out of personal initiative (stages 4, 5, and 6) comprise the rest, about one fourth of his congregation.

When telling me about his efforts to improve his preaching and the church's educational program, he said that he needed this information seven years earlier. His calculations showed that seventy-five people, over half of his congregation, were stuck in their spiritual growth, and the church's preaching and teaching had not adequately dealt with the maturing dimension of discipleship.

What will he do differently now? "Focus on teachable moments," he said. He will be seeking to match the needs of individuals or groups with appropriate spiritual teaching, questions, testimony, and encouragement. Rather than dealing in a general way with the congregation, he will seek to focus the church's teaching ministry at the point of individual and group needs as determined by his profile.

"Above all else," he said, "I will pray for those teachable moments and the insight to see when they are occurring."

SUMMARY

Through case studies and surveys we have seen the dynamic nature of faith. From the simplest affirmation that "God is great and God is good," to the profoundest commitment of one's life in Christian causes, the essence of Christianity is a faith that is ever growing, ever maturing.

Each of us is on this journey, with those starting out being just as precious in God's sight as those who have walked in the faith for many years. The question is not: Who will be the greatest? Rather, the concern is that believers not be complacent but strive faithfully toward full maturity in the likeness of Christ.

By viewing spiritual development through the eyes of others, we can gain perspective that will not only guide us as teachers, leaders, and parents, but will help us in assessing our own spiritual growth.

LEARNING ACTIVITIES

1. Look at figure 16. In which category of faith would you place yourself? _____
2. Name someone in your church in each category.
    1. _____
    2. _____
    3. _____
    4. _____

    Based on your study of faith development, tell how you would discuss religious issues with each.

    _____
    _____
    _____
    _____

3. How do you think the percentage of persons in each category in figure 17 compares with those in:
    Your church? _____
    Your class or group? _____
4. What suggestions do you have for your church in order to meet the needs of people in each category?

    _____
    _____
    _____
    _____

5. List four family members or friends. Tell what category each is in and describe faith issues each will face in the near future.
    1. _____
    _____
    2. _____
    _____

3. _____
   _____
4. _____
   _____

8
Planning for Faith Development

I think the way you bring people to Christian maturity is to be involved yourself on the faith journey: not happy of being ahead of somebody else and not desirous of somebody who is ahead of you. It is important to accept where you are and to know that you are moving. If you know these two things—where you are and that you are moving— then you are really walking shoulder to shoulder with people growing in the faith.

Male, age 28
Deacon and Bible teacher

In this concluding chapter, I want to suggest ways in which we can involve ourselves and others in the faith journey. Obviously, the growth that occurs is a unique expression for every individual; however, there are many common experiences cited by maturing Christians that appear to provide the greatest potential for continuing development. I have grouped these ideas in three categories: individual, family, and church.

INDIVIDUAL DEVELOPMENT

As one person reported, "Prayer is at the heart of it." Rather than citing prayer as a ritual, however, the focus is more on a reflective style of living. For example, this retired woman said, "The verse of Scripture which says that we must pray without ceasing used to bother me. Then I began to realize that prayer doesn't necessarily have to be a constant, conscious, verbalized set of statements made unto God. It can be a constant awareness of God, a constant communing with him."

This woman, as well as most others interviewed, views reflection on and communion with the Creator and creation as the general focus of her spiritual life. But most of these people also find that *specific* forms of meditation are needed. For example, this lady has a daily devotional period. Others cited prayer times, Bible study, quiet times, personal worship periods, devotional reading, and retreats.

Many persons share these reflective experiences with family members or close friends. Husbands and wives often share, some individuals have prayer partners, and small groups are formed to facilitate reflection and meditation.

Another important practice is regular participation in planned activities of one's religious group. Individuals expressed difficulty in being loners; the fellowship and support gained from as well as given to other Christians seems to have a profound effect on one's sense of purpose and meaning theologically as well as personally. The theological issues would relate to one's concept of church, Christians being the body of Christ, and disciples as the people of God. As one interviewee said, "I love people and I think that this has been a big factor in my spiritual growth. My mother used to say that we know we have passed from death unto life because we love the brethren."

From a personal perspective, active participation in a church serves to meet belonging and security needs. There is a sense of wholeness that envelopes individuals as they invest themselves in a *community* of believers. Christian fellowship is the term used most often to describe this ingredient in spiritual growth.

Despite strong involvement with other Christians, a recurring theme among those affirmed as growing spiritually focuses on personal choice and individual responsibility. Here the faith paradox is most apparent—one lives in and is loyal to the Christian community, yet always balances that commitment with thoughts and deeds growing out of personal conviction. Often this leads individuals to go the second mile incarnating their faith while others may be complacent. And, occasionally, such persons will challenge the thoughts or actions of the larger body, alerting others to issues they consider important.

Although there is great variety in the ways individuals seek spiritual growth, there is one common quality that appears basic for a growing Christian: *a faith perspective that enables one to respond openly to questions and new experiences.* Rather than resisting, this quality facilitates the integration of new learning. Thus an individual gains potential for a greater sense of wholeness and meaning in all facets of life. This faith perspective is individual, yet is developed within and nurtured by one's family and larger Christian community, as described in chapter 2.

FAMILY DEVELOPMENT

Without doubt, the foundation for a growing faith emerges from the nurture and indoctrination experienced in the home. While adults are primarily living and refining their faith, children are being impressed with values and models that will influence thought and behavior for a lifetime.

The home where one spent his or her formative years was the influence cited most often in our study. Most persons felt the religious instruction, the examples of Christian living, and the care and concern of their parents provided maximum opportunity for them to develop a personal faith. The general pattern is pretty much the same, as expressed by this young adult:

When I was a little kid I held my parents' world view pretty much. My teenage years from thirteen to eighteen were filled with rebellion against that world view and just about everything else. Since I was eighteen, I have been finding value in life but not in opposition to my parents. I find myself now affirming many of the same values held by my parents.

Male, age 25

The family and home provide a focal point for natural teaching and testing of the fundamental issues in life. By virtue of the close relationships and daily encounters with meaning and purpose in life, there are unlimited opportunities to assist each other in appropriating beliefs and practices deemed important.

Our interviews point out the clarity with which persons having a high degree of spiritual growth can recall the intentional efforts of parents. For example, a woman sixty-two years old said, "My parents taught us children Bible verses; even when we used to work in the fields, my mama would quote Scripture and have us say it back to her. My parents taught us the Bible by example. They *lived* Christian lives, and that fact has had a great impact on me."

We also found that when an unclear or confused impression of faith is conveyed, this often blocks or retards one's future growth as a Christian. An example of this was reported by a man thirty-two years old who had experienced a yo-yo type spiritual life, moving in and out of the intuitive, literal, and peer stages of faith:

I was raised in a middle-class home. My parents took us to church, but I never saw a lot of love for Jesus expressed. We were raised in a lukewarm church. Up through high school I never knew anyone who spoke of Jesus personally. I heard a lot of witness for the church. . . . Looking back, I was spiritually hungry, though I didn't know it then. I was searching for answers.

I had seen the church and decided there were a bunch of hypocrites there. If what they were saying was really true, why weren't their lives changed? Why weren't they happy? So I rebelled against it; in the next five years I never went to church.

The basic principle of faith development in the home is to be consistent in the beliefs and practices of your religion. The corollary is that religion be a natural part of life in a loving and supportive environment. Such provides a sense of belonging to a subunit that easily fits into the larger families of church and community. The security of belonging and the possession of answers which later can be tested and refined provide appropriate faith education leading toward adulthood.

But there is a problem here. Although 75 percent of parents in a national survey said the home is the most important factor in the religious and spiritual development of the young, less than half of the parents with children under eighteen years old had participated during the last week in any type of shared religious activity in home or church.[1]

Lack of consistency in religious education and the uncritical acceptance of cultural faith create a confusing set of principles which the young adopt. Then, without a clear set of values and practices to test and adapt for their own as they move toward adulthood, there is little potential for a growing faith.

What can we do? Let me give you three general guidelines drawn from our interviews with growing Christians as they reflected on faith development in their families.

TEACH YOUR BELIEFS

Seek to communicate the religious beliefs that are basic to your faith. This may be done formally, as in reading the Bible together, learning Scripture passages, discussing religious issues, or through observance of Christian events like Easter and Advent.

Teaching does not have to be structured, however, to have impact. The informal, unplanned discussions among family members concerning the *cause* and *purpose* of everyday events enable all to partake from and to participate in natural faith experiences appropriate for each person's age.

LIVE YOUR BELIEFS

Living that is consistent with teaching reinforces and demonstrates the spoken and written word. The example of one's life can either confirm or confuse the beliefs which one has sought to convey. Which of these influences—teaching or living—has the greater impact on faith development? Persons interviewed say the living of one's beliefs had the greater influence on them.

Teaching is important, but without example it may be viewed

primarily as information rather than valued as life-guiding influence.

The natural approach to learning is an ongoing cycle of action and reflection. As we teach and live our faith, growth is enhanced as we examine the experiences we have. By focusing on questions, feelings, and new experiences, there is opportunity for enhancing current faith expressions as well as projecting new ones.

What are we learning? This is the focal question. Reflection will provide insight for continual growth and improvement. Our interviewees recalled pleasantly these times of reflection, held usually at the dinner table, around the hearth, or following an event of religious significance.

CHURCH DEVELOPMENT

A person's church is the third major partner in faith development. Fellow believers are the ones who help extend faith beyond the natural boundaries of self and family. Despite the feeling that the family exerts primary influence on faith development, the trend is to look to the local church for assistance.

For example, the Gallup research organization reports that countless families in the United States need help desperately, and the major need is for spiritual help. Many Americans, it seems, belong to the "not quite Christian" category:

They believe, but without strong convictions. They want the fruits or reward of faith, but seem to dodge the responsibilities and obligations. They say that they are Christian but often without a visible connection to a congregation or religious fellowship. The major challenge appears to be a task for the churches as well—how to guide men and women into becoming mature Christian personalities.[2]

Churches are responding by developing specialized programs for families, adding staff specialists for family ministry, building family life recreation centers, providing classes for parents in solving family problems, and numerous other ways.

Rather than focusing on such developments, however, I prefer to share with you suggestions gleaned from the spiritually-growing persons in our study. Their insights, while not polished or scholarly, highlight in a simple, personal way the general activities that have elicited and nourished faith in their lives. In my judgment, it is these basic actions which must be foundational in a church that seeks to be intentional in passing on faith.

I am presenting these ideas in seven functional categories.[3] You then must interpret the specific ways in which your church speaks to the needs in each area.

1. Tell and retell the biblical story.

At the core of Christian faith is the revelation of God in the Bible. It is the insights gained from this material that enable persons to share in the common purpose, traditions, commitments, and practices that are a part of church.

Without exception, this was the number one influence in the lives of growing Christians. For many, as young children they received and learned the biblical story; now as older adults they feel great responsibility for telling the story. They want to pass it on.

Out of these biblical studies a church develops its sense of identity as a congregation of persons called by God to be his special people and to do his special work. At this point there can be no compromise—a faith community must agree on its basic purpose and the authority by which its beliefs and practices are judged. Diversity in interpretation and practice can be valuable for a growing faith, but only when it is founded on basic commitments held by the body.

Without distinctives conveyed by a message told and retold, faith can languish. John Westerhoff puts it bluntly:

Often the church tolerates too great a diversity in essentials and hence has no clear identity. When that occurs faith can neither be sustained or transmitted, and community dissolves into institutional togetherness. Faith can only be nurtured within a selfconscious intentional community of faith.[4]

2. Worship and celebrate together.

Lasting impressions are conveyed as Christians worship and celebrate together. Through regular services and special observances opportunity is given to learn and practice traditional forms as well as current expressions of praise, thanksgiving, petition, and meditation.

Rituals important to the church can be interpreted and reenacted, reinforcing the biblical story and translating it into current, personal experience. Rites such as baptism and the Lord's Supper help us reflect on the continual movement of God in our lives and the significance of being in a covenant relationship.

Communion with God through prayer demonstrates for young and old the verbal communication among God and his people. Responsive readings, personal testimonies, and congregational singing are other means through which believers can communicate with God while sharing faith with each other.

Special occasions often are the memorable times in a congregation's life. Celebrating events such as Easter and Advent, the founding of one's local church, and the beginning of a new mission expands the vision of a congregation beyond its own time and place. Even events such as homecomings, building dedications, teacher recognition days, ordination services, parent-baby dedications, weddings, and funerals create teachable moments for exploring and enlarging faith.

3. Listen to and talk with each other.

Without fail, the church must be community, people, a body. Expressing common purpose and developing a fellowship of caring, sharing, and supportive individuals requires together-ness. Fellowship is the term most of the people in our study used; *koinonia* is the Greek word used in the New Testament. Both describe the ideal situation for nurturing believers, as illustrated in chapter 2.

Koinonia cannot develop without sensitive interpersonal com-munication that involves listening to and talking with each other. But such talk cannot be imposed; it has to happen as the by-product of natural, everyday activities in the congregation's life. Eating, playing, and working together were the most-often cited ways to facilitate open communication among members.

What encourages talking? Openness, reported our inter-viewees, along with a desire to discuss life issues. Most influen-tial in their lives were the Christians who had their own opinions but were open to and accepting of the questions and experiences of others. Conversation that is authentic, that recognizes the worth of other people, and that reaches out to draw others in creates the potential for a nurturing fellowship.

4. Listen to and talk with God.

Balancing the outward expressions of praise, prayer, and fellowship must be times devoted to an infilling of mind and spirit. Listening to God is the way one person explained it. "Being still," another said. Silence. Retreat.

I was impressed by the desire of many persons to spend private time alone with God. But they also expressed great appreciation for the time they spend with other church members in silent prayer and meditation.

Such experiences must be viewed as a hopeful and joyful waiting for God, but this may be difficult without congregational support. As Henri Nouwen suggests:

> In the community of faith we can find the climate and the support to sustain and deepen our prayer and we are enabled to constantly look forward beyond our immediate and often narrowing private needs.[5]

Listening to God, although a private act, has community dimensions as we encourage and support each other.

5. *Perform acts of service and witness.*

I have a favorite way of explaining the responsibilities of discipleship: *Christians are called to be, do, and tell the gospel.* Christian service and witness are at the heart of God's call. Whereas the previous suggestions focused on *being,* this one stresses the spiritual growth that comes from *doing* and *telling.*

The consensus of those interviewed is that there is absolutely no substitute for the influence of a life or of a congregation that naturally and faithfully performs acts of service and witness.

This dimension of congregational life provides chances for relating Christian teachings to all facets of everyday experience. For the young, they may absorb the value and meaning in purposeful activity as they experience faith in action. For the more mature, they may gain a sense of personal fulfillment and clearer interpretation of Christian commitments. All share together the opportunity for reflecting on their experience and for developing a greater sense of fellowship.

Christians who serve and witness together convey impressions that are consistent with the biblical truths they profess; consequently, they not only influence the spiritual development of others but also reinforce and enlarge their own faith as well.

6. *Study and learn about your faith traditions.*

We are products of our past. Current beliefs and practices while adapted for our time are always influenced and perhaps even directed by accumulated knowledge, values, and skills passed from generation to generation. When we choose to follow Christ, therefore, we step into a flow of Christian history—past, present, and future. What we are, what we become, and what we pass on are influenced by understandings we learn from our faith tradition.

Scripture, doctrine, liturgy, architecture, and church polity are just part of the heritage upon which we build faith. A critical task of the church has ever been to clarify and interpret this heritage in order to incarnate a faithful witness for the present.

Part of my concern relates to telling and retelling the biblical story, but there must be more. The message of God that birthed the church must always be a converting message, one that renews and empowers faith and practice in any age. So, to claim our identity, it is essential to know our past; and it is also imperative to interpret how best that heritage relates to present experience and the transformations which Christians must seek to achieve.

Knowing and understanding your faith tradition can give understanding to commitment, depth to perspective, and insight to feelings as you seek to be the people of God and the body of Christ in this time.

7. Expect spiritual growth.

Expectation. Anticipation. That is what these people have. In interview after interview they expressed the conviction that a Christian never stops growing. I found that this was in no way a faith-works situation in which these persons were trying to *earn* faith or approval; rather they act out of conviction. They believe and act, and God blesses.

Spiritual growth is a gift from God to a person's inner spirit. As such it must be evoked, used, and affirmed in the life of the church. As pointed out in chapter 2, individuals need an environment in which they can draw from and contribute to the body's life-giving and growth-producing *koinonia*.

Attitude is contagious. We learn from the spirit, encouragement, and example of others. It is not enough just to *expect* spiritual growth, however. This attitude must *permeate our actions*, influencing the ways we plan, organize, and guide church activities; the ways we teach, preach, and witness; and the ways we seek personally to be mature disciples.

LEARNING ACTIVITIES

Evaluate your spiritual growth activities in each of the following areas. If studying this with a group, discuss your responses and make plans for any changes.

1. *Individual*
   I have been doing: _____

   _____
   _____

   In the future, I would like to: _____

   _____
   _____

2. *Family*
   We have been doing: _____

   _____
   _____

   In the future I would like for us to: _____

   _____
   _____

3. *Church*
   We have been doing: _____

   _____
   _____

   In the future, I would like for us to: _____

   _____
   _____
   _____

For Your Personal Reflection
   In a learning activity for chapter 1, you told where you were in your spiritual growth. Read that now before completing the rest of these personal reflection activities.

4. During this study I have come to see my faith as _____

   _____
   _____

5. Three years from now I would like to see the following changes in my faith: _____

_____

_____

_____

6. I want to influence the faith development of _____

_____

_____

7. I want to make the following commitments regarding my faith and the way in which I will pass it on:

_____

_____

_____

_____

_____

Notes

Chapter 2

1. I reported my thoughts on this in an earlier work, thus this material is adapted from that source: Bruce P. Powers, *Christian Leadership* (Nashville: Broadman Press, 1979), pp. 115-26.

Chapter 3

1. Westerhoff has continued to write in the field. The ideas presented here were first published in *Will Our Children Have Faith?* (New York: Seabury Press, 1976), pp. 89 f.

2. Ibid., p. 99.

3. The ideas presented here have been published in a variety of forms. The most comprehensive is James W. Fowler, *Stages of Faith* (San Francisco: Harper and Row, 1981).

4. The conventional always refers to the *commonly held* beliefs and practices, regardless of conservative, progressive, or other labels. The personal in this stage is always in tension with the conventional expression of faith.

5. James W. Fowler "Stages in Faith: The Structural-Developmental Approach," *Values and Moral Development*, Thomas C. Hennessy, ed. (New York: Paulist Press, 1976), p. 198.

6. James W. Fowler, "Faith Development Theory and the Aims of Religious Socialization," *Emerging Issues in Religious Education*, Gloria Durka and Joanmarie Smith, eds. (New York: Paulist Press, 1976), pp. 196-97.

7. James W. Fowler, "Stages in Faith . . . ," *Values and Moral Development*, p. 201.

8. Ibid., p. 202.

Chapter 4

1. J. Terry Young, *The Spirit Within You* (Nashville: Broadman Press, 1977), p. 157.

2. Ibid., p. 157.

Chapter 5

1. I first introduced this concept in chapter 3, as the learning cycle that undergirds faith development. Here I want to describe the process and explain how it relates to teaching and learning.

2. The material in this section is adapted from work by the author published in *Christian Leadership* (Nashville: Broadman Press, 1979), pp. 61-71.

3. Bruce P. Powers, *Helping People Learn* (Nashville: Broadman Press, 1978), audiotape manual, pp. 14-16.

Chapter 6

1. Adapted from *Living with Preschoolers* (Nashville: Sunday School Board of the Southern Baptist Convention, Oct.-Dec., Vol. 9, No. 1, 1981), pp. 42-43.

Chapter 8

1. George Gallup, Jr., and David Poling, *The Search for America's Faith* (Nashville: Abingdon Press, 1980), pp. 50-51.

2. Ibid., pp. 42-43.

3. I am grateful to Professor John H. Westerhoff of Duke University Divinity School for his help in clarifying these categories.

4. John H. Westerhoff, III, *Will Our Children Have Faith?* (New York: Seabury Press, 1976), p. 52.

5. Nouwen, Henri J. M., *Reaching Out* (Garden City, NY: Doubleday and Company, 1975), p. 109.

Resources

CLAYPOOL, JOHN. *Stages.* Waco, Texas: Word Books, 1977.

DAVIS, COS H., JR. *Children and the Christian Faith.* Nashville: Broadman Press, 1979.

DURKA, GLORIA and SMITH, JOANMARIE (eds.). *Emerging Issues in Religious Education.* New York: Paulist Press, 1976.

———. *Modeling God.* New York: Paulist Press, 1976.

EDWARDS, TILDEN H., *et al. Spiritual Growth.* Washington, D.C.: Alban Institute, 1974.

FOWLER, JAMES W. *Stages of Faith.* Kansas City, Missouri: National Catholic Reporter Publishing Co., 1979. Cassette tapes and manual.

———. *Stages of Faith.* San Francisco: Harper & Row, 1981.

FOWLER, JAMES AND KEEN, SAM. *Life-Maps: Conversations on the Journey of Faith.* Waco, Texas: Word Books, 1978.

FRAZIER, CLAUDE A. (ed.). *What Faith Has Meant to Me.* Philadelphia: The Westminster Press, 1975.

GAGNÉ, ROBERT M. *The Conditions of Learning,* 3rd ed. New York: Holt, Rinehart and Winston, 1977.

GALLUP, GEORGE, JR., AND POLING, DAVID. *The Search for America's Faith.* Nashville: Abingdon Press, 1980.

GLEASON, JOHN J., JR. *Growing Up to God: Eight Steps in Religious Development.* Nashville: Abingdon, 1975.

GOULD, ROGER L. *Transformations.* New York: Simon and Schuster, 1978.

GRIBBON, ROBERT T. *The Problem of Faith-Development in Young Adults.* Washington, D.C.: Alban Institute, 1977.

HENDRIX, LELA. *Extended Family.* Nashville: Broadman Press, 1979.

HENNESSY, THOMAS C. (ed.). *Values and Moral Development.* New York: Paulist Press, 1976.

LATHAM, BILL (ed.). *How to Lead Your Family in Bible Study and*

Worship. Nashville: Sunday School Board of the Southern Baptist Convention, 1981. Learning kit.

LEE, JAMES MICHAEL. *The Flow of Religious Instruction.* Mishawaka, Indiana: Religious Education Press, Inc., 1973.

LEYPOLDT, MARTHA M. *Learning Is Change.* Valley Forge: Judson Press, 1971.

LOSONCY, LAWRENCE J. *Religious Education and the Life Cycle.* Bethlehem, Pennsylvania: Catechetical Communications, 1977.

McCOY, VIVIAN ROGERS, *et al. The Adult Life Cycle.* Lawrence: University of Kansas, 1978.

MALONY, H. NEWTON. *Understanding Your Faith.* Nashville: Abingdon Press, 1978.

MUNSEY, BRENDA (ed.). *Moral Development, Moral Education, and Kohlberg.* Birmingham, Alabama: Religious Education Press, 1980.

MUTO, SUSAN ANNETTE AND VAN KAAM, ADRIAN. *Am I Living a Spiritual Life?* Denville, NJ: Dimension Books, 1978.

NOUWEN, HENRI J. M. *Reaching Out.* Garden City, New York: Doubleday & Co., Inc., 1975.

PHILLIPS, J. B. *Your God Is Too Small.* New York: Macmillan Publishing Co., 1955.

POWERS, BRUCE P. *Christian Leadership.* Nashville: Broadman Press, 1979.

_____. *Helping People Learn: Teaching That Changes Lives.* Nashville: Broadman Press, 1978. Cassette tape and manual.

TILLICH, PAUL. *Dynamics of Faith.* New York: Harper & Row, 1957.

TOURNIER, PAUL. *The Seasons of Life.* Richmond: John Knox Press, 1963.

TRENT, ROBBIE. *Your Child and God.* New York: Harper & Brothers Publishers, 1941.

VAN KAAM, ADRIAN. "Original Calling and Spiritual Direction," *Journal of Ongoing Formation,* Vol. 1, February 1980, pp. 7-40.

WEDEL, CYNTHIA C. *Faith or Fear and Future Shock.* New York: Friendship Press, 1974.

WESTERHOFF, JOHN H., III. *Bringing Up Children in the Christian Faith.* Minneapolis: Winston Press, 1980.

_____. *Will Our Children Have Faith?* New York: Seabury Press, 1976.

WHITE, BONNIE and WHITE, ERNEST. *Your Family: Learning, Loving, Living.* Nashville: Sunday School Board of the Southern Baptist Convention, 1979. Learning Kit.

WHITEHEAD, EVELYN E. AND WHITEHEAD, JAMES D. *Christian Life Patterns*. Garden City, NY: Doubleday and Co., 1979.

WILCOX, MARY M. *Developmental Journey: A Guide to the Development of Logical and Moral Reasoning and Social Perspective*. Nashville: Abingdon Press, 1979.

WILLIAMSON, CLARK M. *God Is Never Absent*. St. Louis: Bethany Press, 1977.